"Jess's authentic yet stark h
families but for all families
ship and into a life of impe
others who need a lifeline i

—**Brenda L. Yoder,** LMHC, counselor, author of *Fledge*

"An inspirational story infused with faith, family values, and true appreciation for the simple things in life—like quality time. This is a beautiful testament to how powerful the right perspective can be in the midst of devastation, loss, and the daily challenges of being a parent and devoted spouse."

—**Laurie Hellmann,** author of *Welcome to My Life*, host of *Living the Sky Life* podcast

"From the trials of stepparenting to the challenges of raising a teenager with special needs to figuring out what foods everyone will eat, Jess and her husband, Ryan, don't mince words, but they do give one another and God credit for making it all work. The Ronnes' story will leave you with hope that you, too, can find reasons to celebrate the extraordinary in your own ordinary life."

—**Ingrid Lochamire,** blogger, speaker, author of *One Man's Work*

"If you're walking through a dark time or are just afraid of what's next, this is the book for you. It will resonate with your own experiences and needs, and you will feel like Jess is a friend walking beside you."

—**Jessie Clemence,** author

"Reading this memoir is like being hugged by a warm blanket. A tattered and torn blanket, for sure—it has been through a lot—but that's what gives it the kind of life wisdom and comfort you're looking for. Sit down by the fire with your friend Jessica and wrap yourself in this book."

—**Ron Deal,** blended-family speaker, therapist, best-selling author of *Building Love Together in Blended Families* (with Gary Chapman) and *The Smart Stepfamily*

"Jessica Ronne shares her story of real grief blended with real grace, hardship, and hope. The words she writes of overcoming trauma and tension are an invitation to every family—blended or not—to just keep living for and through love, even in the midst of loss."

—**Rachel Kang,** author, Founder of Indelible Ink Writers

"Jess shares so generously the three things that have restored and nourished her soul in hopes they will restore others': faith, family, and food. With a deep and honest look into a real-life blended family, this ultimately is a beautiful story of surrender—surrender to God's will, God's plan, and God's timing, especially in the midst of incredible pain."

—**Dr. Lisa Peña,** cofounder of Labeled & Loved, author of *Waiting for the Light Bulb* and *The M.o.C.h.A. Diaries*

"Filled with honesty and heart, Jessica invites us into the deep joys and sorrows of being a parent. Sometimes heart-wrenching and other times hilarious, her accessible storytelling about finding healing in unexpected places is all at once fierce and tender—just like the mother she clearly is."

—**Kayla Craig,** author of *To Light Their Way*, cofounder and host of *Upside Down* podcast

"Jess and Ryan share their heartbreaking stories and how God allowed them to find joy again amid the struggle. Jess pulls out true nuggets of gold at the end of every chapter that you can immediately apply to your life and/or marriage."

—**Stephen "Doc" Hunsley,** MD, Executive Director and Founder of SOAR Special Needs

"Every chapter is more than the telling of a story; we're invited to step into the days and make ourselves at home, to not simply observe but to be present in the midst of the push–pull of simplicity and complexity of faith, love, and family. Jessica weaves memoir, caregiving wisdom, and a little kitchen therapy into a book that is not simply read—it is experienced."

—**Ronne Rock,** mentor, speaker, author of *One Woman Can Change the World*

"Even if you have differing experiences, the feelings discussed within this book are universal. Jessica details her experiences so vividly and honestly—making for a read anyone who has dealt with loss or new life can relate to."

—**Stephanie Hanrahan,** Founder of Tinkles Her Pants

"What a breath of inspiration! Blended families will learn so many tips and tricks, from meal negotiations to holiday traditions and the emotions involved."

—**Brenda Stuart,** coauthor of *Restored and Remarried*, counselor/coach, Marriage Illustrators, GilandBrenda.com

"This book resonated in deep places and pulled me through with threads of faith, hope, and love."

—**Gina Kell Spehn,** cofounder and President of New Day Foundation for Families, author of *The Color of Rain*

"An honest, vulnerable reflection about the realities of family life, this book is filled with practical tips for finding joy and balance amid the complexities of marriage and parenting."

—**Kate Motaung,** author of *A Place to Land*

"There aren't enough people being honest about the difficulties of blending, and there don't seem to be enough resources to help those of us who are in the thick of it. Jessica Ronne has emerged in this space with a refreshingly honest and real look at the challenges of blending families, all the while giving us a peek into the beautiful, redemptive stories God writes when he grafts broken lives together."

—**Davey Blackburn,** Founder of Nothing Is Wasted Ministries, host of *Nothing Is Wasted* podcast

"Jess and Ryan Ronne have passed through great adversity without having been defeated or defined by it and continue to grow together in love. Readers of this book who share in their sufferings will also share in the hope and comfort that God has given them."

—**Stephen Grcevich,** MD, President and Founder of Key Ministry, author of *Mental Health and the Church*

"*Blended with Grit and Grace* invites you into a beautiful story of mingling grief and giggles in the hard and unexpected places of blended families. With the heartfelt compassion of someone who's been there, Jess offers a place to know and be known, as well as a friend to walk with on the road before you."

—**Amy Elaine Martinez,** *Past to Power* radio/podcast host, author of *Becoming a Victory Girl*

"I found this book encouraging, authentic, hope filled, and easy to read. Get this book and be ready to learn how to make your family work."

—**Connie Albers,** podcaster, speaker, author of *Parenting beyond the Rules*

"I loved reading the raw honesty of Jess's story and watching how God continues to move through it to bring resolution, hope, and purpose."

—**Shannon Guerra,** author of *Upside Down*

"Jessica feels like a trusted friend who wants to share her story through the hard-fought wisdom she has learned along the way. My heart was warmed and stirred to think about how I intentionally want to love my family—as well as the blended spiritual family God created and has asked us to love—with grit and grace."

—**Rachael Adams,** host of *The Love Offering* podcast

"Whether your family is blended or not, you will find that Jess's insight and counsel will minister deeply to your body, belly, and, most importantly, soul."

—**Callie Daruk,** author of *What Does God Want You to Do before You Die?*

"Jessica Ronne shares her strenuous and harrowing story of finding love after loss by blending personal examples, intimate details, inspirational anecdotes, practical marriage and parenting tips, and mouth-watering recipes. This hope-filled gem delivers a heaping of grit and grace that will leave you echoing Jess's signature mantra: *just keep livin'!*"

—**Chuck E. Tate,** author of *41 Will Come*

"You will sink into Jess's engrossing stories as you learn about the messy yet redeemable reality of blended families. Jess and Ryan figured out through grit and grace how to navigate a large crew of grieving children, their own grief at losing their spouses, and how to move forward in strength and love and boundaries."

—**Lorilee Craker,** *New York Times* best-selling author of 15 books, including *Anne of Green Gables, My Daughter and Me*

"Jessica shares with wit and joy what our aching souls want to discover: the grit of life does not have to wear us down; it can make us into a beautiful pearl instead. Failed expectations are not the end of our story. There is a joy-filled life after death, pain, and hardship after all."

—**Denise Pass,** speaker, worship leader, podcaster, author of *Shame Off You*

"*Blended with Grit and Grace* is a recipe book for blending two families after the trauma of suffering the loss of one or both parents. The curtain is drawn back, allowing us to see what's real and true in addition to the incredible challenges and struggles they experienced, and continue to face, together."

—**Anna LeBaron,** author of *The Polygamist's Daughter: A Memoir*

BLENDED WITH GRIT AND *Grace*

Just Keep Livin'
When Life Is Unexpected

Jessica Ronne

BLENDED WITH GRIT AND GRACE

Just Keep Livin' When Life Is Unexpected

ISBN 978-1-68426-281-6

Printed in the United States of America

Published in association with Stephanie Alton of The Blythe Daniel Agency, Inc., PO Box 64197, Colorado Springs, CO 80962.

Cataloging-in-Publication Data is on file at the Library of Congress, Washington, DC.

Cover design by ThinkPen Design, LLC
Interior text design by Strong Design, Sandy Armstrong

Leafwood Publishers is an imprint of Abilene Christian University Press
ACU Box 29138
Abilene, Texas 79699

1-877-816-4455
www.leafwoodpublishers.com

21 22 23 24 25 26 27 / 7 6 5 4 3 2 1

To Caleb, Tate, Lucas, Mya, Mabel, Joshua, Jada, and Annabelle, the perfect blend of grit and grace. I'm humbled and honored to be your mom.

To Ryan, I want to hold your hand for the rest of my days. I love you.

To my no-holds-barred girls. You know who you are. Your friendship has carried me a time or two.

And finally, to the One who is able to do exceedingly and abundantly more than I could ever think or imagine; the One knee deep in the mess beside me from the beginning; the One who perfectly orchestrated this crazy, chaotic blend of grit and grace.

CONTENTS

FOREWORD

by Kate Battistelli,
author of *The God Dare: Will You Choose to Believe the Impossible?*

Years ago, I read something Edward Albee wrote in his play *The Zoo Story*. He said, "Sometimes it's necessary to go a long distance out of the way in order to come back a short distance correctly."

I could never fully understand it because I heard it before I'd lived it. Now? I understand *perfectly*. I learned the hard way that God's not a genie in a bottle; and he's not a Magic 8-Ball. He is not required to give me everything I want like some kind of cosmic vending machine; and sometimes, he'll take us a long distance out of the way in order to bring us back a short distance correctly. In fact . . . he will dare us to trust just as he did with Jess and Ryan when they acted in faithful obedience through the blending of their families in 2011.

I don't come from a blended family and don't have one now, so I'm not familiar with all the ups and downs that Jessica Ronne has dealt with in her lovingly crafted book, *Blended with Grit and Grace*; but one thing I *do* understand is the pain of loss. For me, it happened through miscarriage and numerous failed adoption attempts.

I'm the crazy woman who longed for five children—with all the crayons, crumbs, and craziness—but God's plan for me was *one child*. It took me *years* to get it through my thick head, and during those years, I found myself consumed by bitterness, depression, and anger toward God.

I'd been taught God was a good Father who gave you the desires of your heart, and my desires were good, for Pete's sake. I wanted a big family, so I relentlessly reminded him that I'd raise my children to know and love him, to follow him all the days of their lives, to honor and serve him. What on earth was I doing wrong? Why wouldn't he give me what I wanted?

Eventually, I figured out he had a different dream for me and my husband—not one we would have chosen. Just like he had a different dream for Ryan and Jess—a dream that would fulfill his perfect plan in their lives like he fulfilled his perfect plan in mine.

Our daughter began revealing gifts and talents that astounded us, and God began to show us how to dig deep and bring out those gifts, polish them up, and offer them to the world.

We were always eager to hear Francesca's newest songs; and as she grew, her songwriting and performing ability grew too, and God began to show this mama's heart he had big plans for our little girl—big plans that would include a future Grammy Award! We didn't know at the time how deeply her songs would affect so many people, one of whom being Jess as she went through intense trials with her son's special needs and her late husband's cancer battle.

As parents, we hope and pray our children's lives will have an impact on other lives; we hope they'll make a difference in the world, but what an incredible blessing it's been to see our child's life and music, her love of Jesus Christ and public worship make such an indelible impact on others' lives! It truly is like "sunlight burning at midnight!" as Jess describes in her memoir.

In my pain, I forgot one little detail in my walk with the One who counts the hairs on my head, the fearful and wonderful maker of the stars above. I forgot this inescapable truth: *It's not about me.*

In my time of deep trial, he taught me three main truths I've treasured and tried to remember as other trials have come:

- He has a bigger plan than my happiness.
- He is thinking about the next generation.
- He wants me to want him for who he is, not what he gives.

God's ways of maturing us into his sons and daughters will always come as a surprise. He chastens to bring change. He will make me face *myself* in the midst of my greatest challenge and see who I really am and how desperately I need him! Isn't that how it always goes when we walk by faith and not by sight?

Be reassured as you read these inspiring words about love, family, marriage, children, and yes, grief and loss: you are on the right path. Life is filled with twists and turns, and we don't know where it's going to take us, but let me encourage you with this, especially if you're young: the years give perspective you may not have now.

You will find lots of wisdom in these pages. Jessica and Ryan have walked the walk—they've faced discouragement and hardships, devastating difficulties with a special-needs son, blending two families with love and laughter—and they've made it work beautifully. They reveal a deep love and respect for one another that's refreshing to discover, and you can almost smell the wonderful dishes Jess is cooking up in her kitchen! Like Jess, I too find solace in the chopping and sautéing and stirring. So, give yourself some grace. Hang in there. Hold tight to the One who's holding you.

By the way, I never had five children, but God did give me five grandchildren, and I couldn't be more thrilled! I get to enjoy plenty of crayons, crumbs, and chaos. My five little peppers who have a Mimi and Poppy devoted to them to the moon and back.

And today I'm grateful, so very grateful, that he *took me a long distance out of the way in order to bring me back a short distance correctly.*

—Kate Battistelli

INTRODUCTION

Growing up I never thought, *When I get older, it would be great to be part of a blended family.* No, this thought never crossed my mind, and why isn't this an aspiring dream for most? Because, first, a blended family is created from a broken family, and this isn't a life goal many pursue; second, most people don't wish difficulties upon themselves! No one anticipates the implosion of the traditional family unit by death or divorce, and when this traumatic occurrence erupts, a plethora of emotions are experienced, including anger, sadness, relief, and depression. However—hallelujah, there is a *however*!—as the dust settles on these experiences of pain, suffering, and misery, something interesting often occurs. We find a new normal. A new dream that seems to work. Perhaps we meet a special someone, which may eventually lead us to the altar, where we will vow to love, honor, and cherish this perfect individual forever and ever.

Suddenly the shattered road doesn't feel so overwhelming, and we turn a sharp, unexpected corner where we discover a freshly paved road. The sun is shining, and the birds are chirping. This new, redemptive existence is joy filled, but it is also a road marked with a unique set of difficulties and challenges—for this is a journey not for the faint of heart.

Hi! I'm Jess. I grew up in a large family in Grand Rapids, Michigan. I attended college, married my husband Jason at twenty-two, had a child in 2002, and began building a grown-up life. We invested in a fitness center, built a house, raised our son, and I discovered I was pregnant again in 2004. Our baby was given a terminal prognosis during a routine ultrasound appointment, but God had a different plan for his fragile life—a story I tell in my memoir *Sunlight Burning at Midnight*.

My plan—oh, don't you love the plans we make—included working part-time, having two more children (a boy and a girl), and being a supportive wife as Jason built his career. What a great idea, right? But . . . there's always a but . . . God had a different plan. Three years later, Jason was diagnosed with a brain tumor. That tumor was not malignant, but the next one, a year and a half later, would be. He lost his battle to cancer on August 24, 2010, and I became a thirty-three-year-old widow with four young children (yes, another boy and one girl). My plan was totally blown to smithereens.

A few months later, on a lonely Halloween night, a blog follower unexpectedly left a comment suggesting I check out a young widower's website. Ryan Ronne lived in Oklahoma with three young children and had recently lost his wife to brain cancer four days after Jason had passed away. I left him a short message, and the rest is history.

We were married in April 2011, adopted each other's children, and went on to have a final child together in 2015—to make it eight—Caleb, Tate, Lucas, Mya, Mabel, Joshua, Jada, and Annabelle. And just like that, I was part of a blended family.

I've now been a mom and wife in this family for ten years, and as with any family, there are joys and trials. Ryan and I didn't initially realize how many complexities there were to consider when blending our family: adoption, special needs, faith, food, traditions, cultures, in-laws, extra-laws, and bylaws, to name a few! The list was exhaustive, and only compounding the difficulties was our daily reality of nine grieving people. To say we were floundering in those first few years is an understatement.

I often sought counsel from women who were many years ahead of me in a successful blended family, and they would suggest making self-care a top priority. Self-care is different for each individual but should be a priority nonetheless. Some might enjoy reading, others working out, shopping, or starting a Bible study, but for me, the concept usually involves food.

One way I unwind after a long stressful day is in the kitchen—cooking, sipping a glass of chardonnay, and listening to soothing music as I chop and dice and sizzle my way through making a meal. Not only is the art of cooking comforting, but it also provides me with tangible activities (slicing, dicing, and sipping) as I mentally wrestle with feelings of insecurity, jealousy, anger, or sadness. Cooking is a healing balm, a therapy for my heart and mind, and has brought me to a place of peace numerous times. Cooking is also a way I can serve and love my family well—by providing nutritious meals that are enjoyed around the table.

My love of cooking has arisen out of a love for food—appreciating new tastes, textures, and cultures—but I wasn't a passionate cook, or honestly a very good one, until we moved to rural Tennessee. I love pizza, pasta, sushi, turkey burgers overflowing with pickled ginger, brisket sandwiches, chicken salad on homemade bread, and warm apple pie straight from the oven, topped with freshly churned vanilla bean ice cream. I love it all, and unfortunately, where we lived, most of my favorites were not readily available. If I was going to enjoy the foods I loved so dearly, I had to learn to make them, one way or another.

As I navigated the art of cooking, I taught myself through trial and error. I added or subtracted certain ingredients, often opting for healthier alternatives such as honey for sugar or applesauce in place of oil—tweaking and adjusting until the finished product was delicious and offered nutritional value to my family.

Ryan and I approach life in a similar way—tweaking and adjusting to accommodate different needs, cultures, traditions, and personalities in an effort to create a cohesive, well-oiled machine—a family thriving in a healthy environment. We've had difficult conversations and celebrated the differences we each bring through our varied backgrounds and experiences.

Cooking through the stressful phases of life provides me with an escape from the daily grind of motherhood, which came in especially handy when I instantaneously added three children to my brood. Raising seven—and later eight—little people is not easy. Admittedly, I entered our blended family with ignorance. I naïvely reasoned that as the eldest of twelve kids, how difficult could it really be? I'm here to tell you, it is hard. I blundered and triumphed and lost my cool time and time again through those first years, but the kitchen remained steady. It beckoned me. It promised a safe, soothing haven—a refuge, as I shooed the kids out (yes, I'm that mom), turned on the music, and poured myself a glass of wine. Cooking brings me peace, which leads to joy, as I slowly stir a big pot of beef stew or add more stock to the chicken curry simmering away on the back burner. The repetitive motions remind me that life takes time, as does anything worth having.

As long as we continuously stir the pot, have the conversations, check in with one another (and ourselves) about how pressure is affecting our emotional well-being, say I'm sorry and I love you, and of course, forgive often, it will come together—with time—forming something deeply redeeming and beautiful. Many of my favorite slow-cooking dishes represent my family and the stories of our life together. Each ingredient, raw in its original form—chicken, veggies, broth, spices, herbs, maybe a little fruit—may be unique, yet each lends to the flavor of the dish, to the art of the finished product. However, the delicious result is only obtained through the steady, low flickering flame of the burner or the warm oven, as the individual ingredients meld together into a meal.

Within each chapter, there's a theme related to our blended life, with stories detailing how we've dealt with obstacles, issues, and the triumphs we've encountered thus far in our ten years of marriage. Although this book is primarily written from my perspective, Ryan—the father and husband of this whole kit and kaboodle—also chimes in throughout as he offers a uniquely male take on our unexpected life experience (see the sections titled "Ryan's Take" for his insights). This book also includes a series of key takeaways in the form of quick, easy-to-read, bulleted lists to summarize the discussion and provide you with some helpful tips. Finally, there is a handful of our family's favorite recipes, most of which take time for the true blending of the flavors to develop—just as our family has taken time to blend and mature. What you won't find within these pages are all the answers, and we don't claim to have it figured out. These are our stories, solutions that worked for us, and they may or may not work for others. Let this book serve as a good friend who listens during a difficult time. It won't offer an onslaught of advice but instead seeks to be supportive—nodding in agreement—*Yes, it's a difficult road, but you will get through it and there is abundant joy if you stay the course.*

My hope is that you, dear reader, feel less alone on your unexpected journey, that you can laugh and learn from many of our mistakes (and triumphs!), and perhaps bring your family closer together as you attempt to create one or two of the dishes presented throughout.

I pray you open your heart, mind, and of course, your mouth not only to engage in healthy honest communication with the people you love but also to take a few minutes to slow down, share a meal, and enjoy some good ole cooking simmering away on the back burner of your stove. Just keep livin'!

1

OUR NEW, BLENDED FAMILY

Releasing *Expectations* and Embracing *Reality*

Savannah, Georgia, is where it all began. Ryan and I met in this beautiful historic city in December 2010—four months after the deaths of our spouses. After weeks of emails, texts, and calls, we decided that the time had come to meet face to face. Neither of us wanted the initial meeting to occur in our home states, and we excluded the children until we knew that the relationship was moving forward. We settled on Georgia, a state on our bucket lists—a slow, southern land of warmth and sweet tea.

I booked various trusted friends, sitters, and family members to care for my kids as I prepared to meet Ryan, a man I had admittedly fallen in love with over the course of a few weeks—a man I had only talked to via emails, texts, and phone calls. Sounds like a creepy episode of *Dr. Phil*, huh? The night before I was scheduled to leave, I couldn't sleep. I tossed and turned as constant doubts bombarded my thoughts: *Will he be handsome? Will he be attracted to me? Will we connect? Will my kids be okay while I'm gone? Will I be taller than him?*

That last question worried me.

Ryan had assured me that he was 5'11" to my 5'10", but I had some concerns. I did not want to tower over a potential future husband.

The morning finally arrived, bright and early. I greeted my mom—the first of the caregivers—and she gave me a tight squeeze and told me to have fun.

At the airport, I settled in with a magazine and my phone vibrated. I glanced down: *I can't wait to meet you in a few hours.*

My heart leapt—a message from Ryan.

I responded: *I can't wait to meet you too.* And then I smiled at the thought of how close I was to meeting a man I was quite certain I was already in love with.

When boarding began, I joined the line, eager yet with nerves getting the best of me as I struggled to calm my beating heart. In less than two hours I would meet who I hoped would be the man of my dreams, and before I knew it, the plane was descending into Savannah. I stood up, had a good stretch, collected my belongings, said a little prayer, and headed in the direction of the baggage claim where he and I had agreed to meet.

Ryan's plane landed twenty minutes after mine, so I quickly called my girlfriend Tara, who was rooting for me from Michigan: "Tara! I'm freaking out!" I whispered. "I can't stop shaking—I'm so nervous!"

"Jess, calm down. Take it one step at a time. First things first. Meet him and then call me!"

As I hung up the phone, I turned, and there he was. My dream guy, Ryan, walking toward me with a huge smile. He looked incredibly handsome in jeans and a rustic baseball cap, and he immediately engulfed me in a huge embrace. I held on for dear life to this stranger I had adored from the first words in our emails and now face to face—his face slightly (by an inch) taller than mine. Praise Jesus for small victories and expectations fulfilled.

Our weekend was romantic as we talked and kissed and wined and dined to our heart's content. We pored over memories—discussing "them," our late spouses, Jason and Kaci—as we shared pictures and histories and lives spent with other people. These individuals we had loved and had created families with. People who were now in heaven. We were completely engrossed with one another—so much so that the whole world could have blown away and I'm not sure we would have noticed, at least until our last night together.

We dined somewhere that final evening. I'm sure it was beautiful, and I'm also sure we hardly ate because the endorphins of new love sustained us in those early days. We roamed the cobblestone streets and then returned to the hotel, where we cozied up in Ryan's room to watch a movie on his laptop. As we cuddled together, all snuggled up nice and close, *she* appeared on the screen. A video of Kaci, Ryan's late wife, flashed before our eyes in the middle of the movie. Not as a ghost but instead as an old recording that for some unexplainable reason started playing during our romantic time together. Talk about killing the mood. I immediately backed away from my new boyfriend—hurt and confused and now very aware of this other woman who had been a part of his life. She was no longer a vague idea, a stranger in a photo, but was now a reality with mannerisms and a personality and a southern drawl. A reality who Ryan had been married to. Had he planned this? Were we not supposed to be together? Was God sending us a message?

Ryan repeatedly apologized, and I assured him that it wasn't a big deal, but it did feel like a big deal. We had entered Savannah with a fantasy idea that we would be enough for each other and that somehow our love would erase the grief we had, but when I saw her, I realized that I couldn't be enough and that Ryan couldn't erase my pain either. There was grief we had to face in order to move to the other side of our respective losses. In time. It was a strange and confusing place to be—falling in love with one person while simultaneously grieving another—but it was where we were, and we had to own our unique paths.

We were heartbroken saying our goodbyes the next morning. Our love was real but so was our grief, and in saying goodbye, it felt like another loss. We knew that God had placed our families on a path of redemption, and on that path, there would be numerous opportunities to release our preconceived expectations and embrace our blended reality, which would have a few hiccups—one that involved the bright red pots that adorned my kitchen shelves when we were married that following spring.

Red Pots: Embracing Our New Life through Difficult Conversations

In the beginning, there was a couple. This pair of lovebirds named Jessica and Ryan flitted about in bliss and romance, and then something hit them one day—like a nosedive straight into a freshly Windexed window. *Bam!* The couple was stunned silly as they shook off rose-colored blinders, unruffled their feathers, and saw what everyone else had been seeing all along—reality. Reality came close to shattering our romantic naïveté in little ways those first few months of marriage; minor missteps we quickly forgave because our love was blissful and new. However, approximately five months postwedding, I ventured into the kitchen and opened a cupboard to retrieve a cooking pot. I reached for one of my new pots, which I inherited from Ryan's former household—a bright-red Teflon pot. Now, personally, I don't believe Teflon is a safe product. But here was this Teflon pot in my cupboard, at my husband's insistence. Next to other colorful Teflon pots, which he had packed into our cupboards. I cringed as I always had since those pots had been placed there months earlier. Then it happened. I decided: *No more red pots!*

Before our wedding, I flew to Oklahoma to help Ryan pack for his move to Michigan. I honestly had no idea what a disaster I was about to behold. I occasionally joke about how my husband has a tiny bit of a pack-rat mentality, and this is what I faced upon arrival. We began in the basement, where we rummaged through hundreds of boxes. I finally threw my hands up and suggested we pack it all and organize the contents later. This was not the best idea, because once in Michigan, our home would be large enough to accommodate his numerous belongings. And when I say *his* belongings, I am referring to *their* belongings—his late wife and himself. Pictures, knickknacks, casserole dishes, silverware, pots and pans, and anything else you can possibly imagine. Fortunately, they were well cared for. Most were fairly new and in great condition; however, I didn't like many of them. This can be a touchy subject. Typically, a woman who remarries doesn't want belongings from her husband's previous marriage to have a prominent place throughout her new home. There is something about making a home personal, and incorporating another woman's possessions isn't at the top of that agenda. This tendency, I'm certain, is in part tied to insecurity—especially in a new marriage, as the years and shared experiences haven't had the opportunity to solidify trust in the relationship.

Back to the red pots—I also don't like bright colors. My decorating style veers toward neutrals, and I was resentful that *my* house was full of décor that made me cringe. In my previous marriage, I decorated according to what I liked. My late husband Jason didn't have an opinion about how I accomplished this, what I purchased (as long as it was within the budget), or what color dishes we had. But Ryan seemed to have an opinion about everything, and this irritated me. I began thinking and praying about it—but mostly thinking about it—and decided my mental well-being was more important than holding on to anything that brought me angst. I packed a big cardboard box with belongings I no longer wanted—yes, including the Teflon pots—and marked it for Goodwill. When Ryan saw the box, he began to ask questions, and soon the conversation spiraled into a full-blown argument.

"Why would you give these pots away?" he asked.

I had been stewing for months and convincing myself that my husband was attached to these dumb red pots. My head was filled with lies: *He just wants his old life back. He isn't ready to marry me. He doesn't even love me!* Needless to say, my husband was in for a treat. I explained, not so calmly: "These pots make me feel like you regret marrying me and want your old life back. I have these belongings all over *my* house that I don't want! I don't like bright colors or Teflon, yet I have colorful Teflon pots in my cupboards! And all of it belonged to another woman whom you were in a relationship with. Your wife! Which is unsettling because I'm your wife. It isn't right."

I continued to explain how I was slightly territorial and wanted to be the only woman in his present life, and as long as I had a household full of another woman's belongings—belongings that I didn't care for—I was going to struggle emotionally, especially in a new relationship where I was dealing with feelings of insecurity. I explained how I needed the red pots to be gone for my peace of mind. Home is my refuge, but with someone else's décor splattered throughout, it didn't feel homey or safe. It felt like I was living in another woman's reality.

Ryan was genuinely surprised as my true feelings emerged and couldn't fully understand my reasons for attempting to dispose of his belongings simply because I didn't like them. In his defense, this is completely out of character for me, as I am generally grossly opposed to wastefulness. As we communicated, it became clear the red-pot issue had to do with his upbringing more than anything else.

Ryan's Take

Jess is correct. I grew up with limited possessions, so anything I purchased was earned and was therefore valuable. To earn extra money, I even started dumpster diving around five years old! I quickly became a pro and was diving solo by eight years old. The neighborhood kids and I would walk miles of alleys as I learned which trash bins to hit and when. We collected aluminum cans, and when I heard loud music a couple of houses down from ours late into the night, I wasn't concerned by the lack of sleep. I was estimating how much money I would have the next day.

I did have a slight emotional attachment to the red pots that I wasn't willing to admit because I generally try to avoid conflict. They were one of the few thoughtful, expensive gifts I had purchased my late wife. That was one of the reasons for my disdain when I saw them packed, not so neatly by the way, in a random Goodwill box. I saw the red pots as a huge upgrade for Jess, since most of her cookware had been purchased at secondhand stores and garage sales. I love a good bargain, but I truly thought she would eventually grow to like them if she used them long enough. As a man, I couldn't understand why it mattered where they came from, and at that point in our marriage, I still considered them mine. I had no idea the inner turmoil she was going through over what I considered a minor irritant; however, I learned to understand it wasn't really about the red pots and more about her feeling like I was bringing pieces of my previous marriage into our marriage.

> When it comes down to it, time really does heal—even when it came to the red pots and many other misunderstandings in those first years.

It's important to have the difficult conversations. It can be incredibly awkward to be the person who brings an issue to the surface, but these feelings must be aired out before bitterness begins to fester. We make these conversations less painful by choosing a time when neither of us is distracted or enjoying a rare moment of peace. If Ryan brings up an issue while I'm making dinner, I'm going to be frustrated. If I bring up an issue as he's packing for a relaxing day of fishing, that's going to defeat the purpose of his relaxing day because all he'll be thinking about is the issue. We've also learned to tackle one problem at a time. I have more difficulty in this area. That time he tracked mud into the house leads to the time he didn't help with dishes, which leads to that one time, five years ago, when he didn't want to get rid of the red pots. I'm learning to train my thoughts and stay on point for the sake of harmony and respect within our marriage.

These conversations have helped our family, as we bridge the transition between expectations and the reality that calls for grace in certain circumstances—even in the face of colorful Teflon pots.

Mom and Momma: Releasing Expectations

"It makes me so angry that I call your dad 'Dad' and you won't call my mom 'Mom'!" screamed seven-year-old Caleb to his brother Tate a few weeks into our new life together.

Although Caleb and Tate were only six months apart and shared the experience of losing a parent at a young age, their lives had been vastly different up until that point. Caleb had been my right-hand man for three years as his father fought cancer. He cared for his younger siblings, brought his dad meals in bed, and processed the hair loss, nausea, and goofy words that escaped Jason's lips while brain cancer ravaged away his sensibilities. He witnessed and ultimately came to an acceptance of his father's death before Jason officially gained his citizenship in heaven, and he was the one who found his father lifeless only minutes after he had breathed his last. He worked through the stages of grief: denial, anger, bargaining, depression, and finally acceptance simply by being in the turmoil. He often voiced what Jason and I had feared—"Is Dad going to die?"—and, in turn, he forced us to look at the truth, stripping away the pretenses or fallacies we were clinging to. He drew pictures of himself and Jason in heaven and placed them beside his pale, motionless father while he slept. Caleb was given the gift of time—time to face the possibility that his father would not always be with him—and he used that time to grieve. Now he was eager to welcome a new father figure into his life. The first time he met Ryan, he asked if he could call him Dad because he desperately yearned for a father again.

Ryan's Take

Kaci was unexpectedly diagnosed with a brain tumor in March 2010. The family knew she would be doing radiation treatments for the next six weeks, so we each took a turn staying with her since the treatments were hours from home. I went first and then returned home to be with the kids.

However, only days into her treatments, the tumor hemorrhaged and everything changed. I spent the next six weeks in and out of the hospital, and the rest of the time, we stayed in a long-term hotel so she could be close to the neurologist. Tate, Mya, and baby Jada were primarily cared for by Kaci's mom and didn't witness their mother's quick decline. They occasionally visited but didn't realize she had the dreaded C-word—cancer—until a few weeks before she died. They enjoyed grandma's house, as grandmas typically offer a looser set of rules, and they basked in their newfound freedom. They viewed the experience as a prolonged, fun vacation, and when Mom regained her health, they would return to their life with rules, chores, and responsibilities. They weren't processing their feelings or working through any stages of grief.

Kaci and I ended up in Houston's Johns Hopkins Cancer Treatment Center in July 2010, where they did an MRI and discovered that the tumor had grown roots, encapsulating her entire spinal cord. As the doctors shared this news with me, I finally accepted that her time was up. I made a few phone calls, and she and I went home.

I sat down with my kids during the last week of Kaci's life and prepared them for the reality of her death. I'm sure they were confused and knew something was wrong as they sat nervously on the floor beside me. I told them that their mom was declining and that the cancer had gotten worse. As the C-word escaped my lips, Tate immediately went rigid and proclaimed, "Dad, Momma doesn't have cancer. She only has a tumor." I explained that her tumor was cancer. I realized then that Tate knew people recovered from tumors but they died from cancer, and he cried for the first time since her diagnosis. We all cried as I informed them that mom didn't have much time left, but she wanted to spend what time she had at home. She died less than a week later—only four months after she had been a healthy, normal momma to her three children.

While Caleb had reached acceptance after three years, Tate had just begun his journey with grief. I was also in denial, which delayed the grieving process, so I was shocked when a few weeks after Kaci's death, Tate asked, "Dad, will we get another mom soon?"

That question made me face reality. I was a thirty-three-year-old widower with a seven-year-old, a five-year-old, and an eight-month-old baby. I knew I didn't want to raise them alone, but I had no idea what God had in store or how quickly our lives would change.

So, what's in a name? We never pressured or asked the kids to call us anything, and we allowed them to pave their individual paths. Each one chose to call us Mom or Dad, except for Tate. We figured he would call me Mom in his own time, if ever, but I was hopeful that we would eventually get to that place in our relationship.

He and I got along great and even bonded in our first few months together. He affectionally called me Jessica, while the other kids immediately took to calling me Mom and Ryan Dad. It seemed to work until we heard Caleb yelling at Tate over the situation.

Caleb felt like I was being rejected by his new brother, whereas he had accepted his new dad, Tate's dad—and this wasn't fair. Caleb was fighting for me, which was sweet, but it was a misguided battle.

I pulled Caleb aside for a chat.

"Why does it bother you so much that Tate won't call me 'Mom'?" I asked

"Because your kids call Dad 'Dad,' and Mya and Jada call you 'Mom,' so Tate should too," he explained.

"Honey, Tate can call me 'Jessica' if he wants to. He's not at the same point in the grief process as you are, and it might take time for him to work through his feelings—and that's okay."

Caleb's personality dictates that he needs an explanation to process experiences, and once he receives this valuable information, he's able to lend more grace to almost any situation. He was still frustrated but understood the reason Tate was hesitant to call me Mom.

Ryan's Take

While Jess was trying to explain things to Caleb, Tate and I also had a heart-to-heart. He wasn't ready to call Jess Mom because he felt like that meant he had to say goodbye to his birth mom. I helped him understand that he never had to let go of her memory, and she would always be his momma. He needed permission to love and accept a new mom, and to feel like he wasn't replacing his momma by accepting Jess. Kaci would always be Momma and Jess could be Mom—two separate women. There could be room for both in his heart.

It didn't take more than a few days for Tate to ask, "Mom, can I go see if the neighbors can play?" or "Mom, what's for dinner?" It was a little awkward initially, but as we gained confidence and momentum in accepting our lives together, "Mom" slipped off his tongue just as easily as "Momma."

The name game can be tricky to navigate when you're first starting out as a newly blended family. Ryan and I have messed up numerous times in how we've addressed issues, but I think we got it right here. We let the kids lead and had vulnerable conversations as we explained that acceptance doesn't mean you're letting go of what came before. Acceptance simply means you've reached a place of allowing more love to grow in your heart. Tate had to hear that he could keep "Momma" for Kaci, and if you find yourself in the same situation, maybe your child needs to keep a name sacred for someone as well. It may be Momma, or Gigi, or Daddy. Allow this. Allow for time and healing. Give your child space to process. Some kids will be on board immediately with a new mom or dad figure, and others may take years to get to that place. It's not a reflection of you as a person, and miraculously, I didn't take it that way here as I so often do in other situations. It's also not a rejection of you as a parent. It's simply a reflection of the child's need for time, healing, and acceptance—an invaluable lesson my sister taught me early on in life.

Sisters: The Importance of Choosing Acceptance

I grew up with adopted siblings, and during childhood, I had no idea how this experience would one day shape my life when I adopted Tate, Mya, and Jada.

I was closest in age to my adopted sister Karen, although we were not emotionally close growing up because she entered my life the year I left for college. She had a rough childhood. As a young girl, her mother brought her to a children's home in India when she was unable to care for her. She was later adopted by an American family at age thirteen who didn't understand how to meet her need for love and affirmation, and eventually, her father placed her back in the system after her adopted mother died. Enter my family, who adopted her when she was fifteen years old, but the scars of rejection had already found their place in her young life. Those scars begged for strong doses of affirmation and praise as she continuously sought to answer the questions that beat in her heart: *Do you love me? Do you want me? Or will you abandon me as so many already have?*

As children, we don't understand the complexities of the human soul, and I saw Karen's neediness as taking away from the already limited amount of personal attention we received from our parents. I prided myself on not being needy like her and resented that she was always seeking affirmation as she struggled to trust that those who were supposed to care for her wouldn't leave her again.

I never thought twice about the decision to adopt Tate, Mya, and Jada. Maybe I should have given it more thought, as it was a life-changing decision, but it came down to falling in love with Ryan and seeing a need. He was a father to three motherless children. I loved him and loved his kids by proxy. It made sense to remedy their void by becoming their adopted mom. I have never regretted my decision; however, I will admit that I entered it very naïvely and have struggled through significant emotions as I dealt with the aftermath of this life-changing role.

Shortly after the ink on the adoption papers had dried—about a year into my marriage—I began to suffer from depression. I missed my biological children. I had devoted three years to caring for Jason, and then months cultivating a marriage and forming bonds with three new children. I realized I had put my biological kids on the back burner, convinced they would be okay because they innately knew my love for them. I was their mom!

I had a deep ache for Caleb, Lucas, Mabel, and Joshua, but I wasn't sure how to remedy this desire without the other kids feeling slighted. My expectation was that bonds would simply fall into place—the connections with Tate, Mya, and Jada would magically appear—but they didn't. It was natural to reach for Joshua, who I had carried in my belly for nine months and who lovingly gazed into my eyes as I held him. It wasn't natural with Jada, who often eyed me with suspicious contempt when I reached for her. I knew that depth in relationships took time, but I didn't want to cause my children any more pain than they had already experienced. I often pulled attention from my biological kids and gave it to my adopted ones, and then one day I simply broke. Ryan found me hunched over our desk as tears streamed down my face.

"I miss my kids!" I blubbered as the emotions of the past year rose to the surface.

"Honey, you can miss your kids," he gently replied.

"But I don't want your kids to think that I love my biological kids more than I love them," I replied.

He continued: "Your relationship with Caleb, Lucas, Mabel, and Joshua is deeper, and my relationship with Tate, Mya, and Jada is deeper. That's the reality. All you can do is bond with each child in small ways to build connections with him or her."

His words opened a door for me that day. He gave me permission to say, "It is different. It's different for me, and it's different for them, and that's okay."

Ten years later, my relationship with all the kids has solidified and deepened, as relationships do with time. My sister Karen has become an invaluable resource and friend as I navigate the tricky world of adopted feelings and concerns. She has served as a sounding board for the abandonment and attachment issues that often present in adopted children, and she's offered advice on tactics and skills to try. She continues to teach me valuable lessons in grace through how she navigates her own experience, and I now see our blended family as a beautiful illustration of how our heavenly Father chooses us in our insecurities, unmet expectations, and imperfect histories, and simply loves us as his children.

A few years ago, Karen and her kids made the long journey to Tennessee from Michigan. We spent time laughing, watching the cousins play together, and of course, cooking. The beauty of having a sister from India is that she is gifted at cooking curry! During our visit, we spent a good portion of our time in the kitchen, where she taught me the authentic way to make chicken curry. This dish involves a lot of slicing and dicing and throwing the ingredients into a big pot, then simmering them on low heat for hours on end. Kind of like our family—the individuals slowly blend through intentional time together and meaningful connections. However, there is another important component to a blended family, a difficult aspect that we'll discuss in the next chapter: You might need an extra-sharp knife for the type of slicing and dicing that might occur. I'm talking about creating healthy boundaries—boundaries that often involve removing aspects, traditions, or possibly even relationships that aren't beneficial or uplifting to the new marriage or family. Sometimes, difficult decisions must be made for growth and life to occur.

This dish is comfort food at its finest, especially during the cooler autumn and winter months, and it's full of healthy nutrients that will start your family off right during the cold and flu season. You'll feel like the parent of the year as you dole this out on your family's plates.

- 1 large onion, diced
- 4–5 garlic cloves, diced
- Olive oil
- 1–2 large jalapeños, diced (remove seeds for less spice)
- 2 28-ounce cans of chopped tomatoes
- 4–5 chicken thighs, cut into pieces
- 7–8 cups of chicken or bone broth
- 2 cans of chickpeas, drained and rinsed
- 1–2 tbsp curry powder
- 1 tbsp cumin
- 1 tsp chili powder
- Salt and pepper to taste

Sauté the onion and garlic with the olive oil on medium heat until translucent. Add the jalapeños and cook for a minute—stirring constantly. Add the tomatoes and broth. Stir. Add the remaining ingredients. Stir and simmer on low all day long, stirring occasionally. Serve over rice or a baked potato.

2

FACING GHOSTS FROM THE PAST

Constructing Healthy *Boundaries* to *Protect* a Marriage

Ryan and I initially brought "them," Kaci and Jason, into our relationship. We moved so quickly in our love that it was bound to happen. I was further along in the grieving process when Ryan entered my life. Jason was diagnosed with a brain tumor in 2007, and I married Ryan in 2011—after four years of intensely wrestling with my faith and God, eventually arriving at the acceptance stage.

But Ryan had received the diagnosis in March 2010 and married me in April 2011. I inadvertently became a big bandage for his pain. Yes, we should have pursued therapy before moving so quickly—or at least therapy in the first year or two of our marriage. But we didn't, and the relationship worked despite our failures.

Jason and Kaci were often subjects of our conversations in those early days. These talks were therapeutic or sometimes a veiled attempt to reveal our desire to avoid particular traits or patterns that were present or ignored with the former spouses. For instance, neither of us went to bed when they did, and we often opted for a later bedtime. Interestingly, neither of us particularly liked this habit and decided not to transfer it to our marriage (and we haven't).

Ryan and I were growing deeper in love by the moment and initially assumed that Jason and Kaci would always be a part of our relationship, but something shifted in the spiritual realm as we took vows to love, honor, and cherish one another until death do us part. *'Til death do us part.* Romans 7:2. This is where the conversation gets tricky. *Their* constant presence being a part of our marriage often led to resentment and heated arguments.

One evening, I presented myself to Ryan after spending a considerable amount of time getting ready—glammed up and ready for a night on the town.

Ryan quickly glanced up from his position on the couch as I walked into the room.

"You look nice," he commented.

"Nice?" I replied, slightly annoyed. "That's not very enthusiastic."

"What's wrong with me saying you look nice?" he questioned. "Do you want me to do cartwheels or something?"

"No, I don't need cartwheels, but I don't understand why you can't be more excited when I do look nice. It's not often, you know. I'm usually in yoga pants and a T-shirt. It doesn't seem like you care."

"I do care honey, but you don't have to get ready for me. You do that for you."

"*What?* You don't even care if I look nice? That doesn't make me feel special."

At this point, it was headed in the direction of a very unenjoyable evening.

"What are you after?" he asked angrily.

"I just don't feel beautiful with you. Jason *always* called me his queen and told me I looked beautiful in anything—even jeans and a T-shirt."

"Well, I'm not Jason," came the defensive reply. "I'm Ryan. Your husband, remember?"

Disclaimer—Jason was wildly outspoken, loud, and extroverted. Yes, this statement aligned absolutely with who he was. Did he *always* go above and beyond to tell me I was beautiful? Not likely. This was probably part of a misguided memory I created to suit myself and my ego.

For whatever reason, I was so narrowly focused on my perception of how Jason *always* treated me that I was willing to jeopardize a romantic night with my husband Ryan.

We managed to talk through most of the angst and have an enjoyable time. I wish I could say all our early arguments ended this smoothly, but they did not. Many nights involved weeping and explosive grief, and it took years of self-care and awareness (and every self-help book written by Kevin Leman) to realize I was hurting the man I was married to, and in the process, I was not serving my current marriage very well with these constant comparisons.

Most of these conversations stemmed from insecurities or jealousies, and some originated from information we never should have shared! There are aspects of our first marriages that should have been sacred to that relationship, not aired out to our new spouses.

We decided that moving forward, we would refrain from involving them in our marriage. This decision was easy when we understood that *they* often caused many of our fights and was reinforced when we searched the Bible for validation. Mark 10:8 states that marriage is when "the two are united into one" (NLT). Not two plus the deceased spouses. Ryan did not marry me and

Jason, and I did not marry him and Kaci. He and I married each other. Yes, our first spouses led us to who we are in our marriage, and without their deaths, we would not be together. Yes, we recognize and honor the role they played in our lives; however, death parted us, in the marital sense, as our vows declared.

Additionally, these types of conversations always seemed to be one-sided, as neither of us knew the other's spouse; plus, the information received arrived through a lens of sainthood. There's an old adage about never speaking ill of the dead, and this can be detrimental in a marriage where there are deceased spouses. Over time, these memories of perfection add up and become a big idol—yes, an idol, and I'm raising my hand high here. First, our memories tend to be inaccurate—statistically, we get 70 percent of our memories wrong, and we often view the past through a distorted lens that suits us. Sometimes Ryan will do something that irritates me or approach a situation in an unfamiliar way, and I've been guilty of thinking: *Jason would never do that. Jason never treated me that way. Jason would have brought me flowers every month.* That last statement is probably a good example of a distorted memory. I've now raised Jason to a status of perfection (idolatry), and possibly, I would dare to suggest, my thoughts are hinging on emotional adultery. I shouldn't be thinking such intimate thoughts about another man. Even one I used to be married to. *Used to.* Back to my vows—*'til death do us part.*

My marriage with Jason ended when he died. I remember the moment I physically felt something rip off me—a part of me—when he took his last breath. I finally exhaled deeply in a feeling that was beyond understanding, and I knew that our marital vows had been completed. I was free to move forward and one day love again.

It's not fair to my current marriage to compare Ryan to a perfect, sainted person whom I have distorted memories about. I imagine it's different in divorce situations. When a divorced couple remarries, I doubt many reminisce about their previous spouse, as that might be awkward. Returning to biblical wisdom—*the two shall become one*. Practically speaking, I have set my former relationship with Jason aside in my heart as something sacred I had with him, a man I loved. My faith tells me that Jason is in all-encompassing love in heaven and has no need for my active love anymore. He is loved eternally by our heavenly Father, as I will be someday, but for my time here on earth, my active love belongs to my one and only—Ryan. It's not only love but respect.

I can hear your thoughts churning about our children, and yes, we approach the kids differently. They didn't have a marital relationship with their parents in heaven, and those relationships are different because there weren't vows involved that involve the spiritual aspect of being a Christian. Ryan and I fulfilled our vows to Jason and Kaci. We loved and cared for them in sickness and in health until death parted us.

Perhaps you are in the process of navigating healthy boundaries in your marriage while facing all the feelings and expectations that arise when we confront ghosts from our past. Here are some helpful takeaways to help you along your journey.

TAKEAWAYS

- Remember: It's "two shall become one"—not "four shall become two."
- When the people we love pass away, they are sainted, and it isn't fair to compare them to a living spouse who is a sinful human being and will repeatedly fail.
- Find a therapist. Really.

- Understand that most of your memories are not entirely true and are remembered through a distorted lens that suits you.
- Focus on the person you're with. All that energy, love, and devotion—shift it to the one you've spoken your vows to. That's the person who needs it.

Ryan's Take

I feel like men generally view the topic of *'til death do us part* differently than women. Even the two words *widow* and *widower* have different connotations. Society is more sympathetic toward widowers, especially when young children are involved. Widowers are often encouraged to find someone to fill the void left by the deceased spouse—sometimes even sooner than they may be ready for! And we are hailed as heroes when we adopt fatherless children, whereas new mothers are often viewed as evil stepmothers. Thank you, Walt Disney, for that perception. I believe I was initially unprepared to move on. As men, we are taught that grieving is a sign of weakness, and I was supposed to get up, dust myself off, and move on with life. But widowers are also romanticized by the world, and the expectation is that we hold an undying love for our late wives through all of eternity

I had been Kaci's caregiver through four months of cancer treatments, but then she died, and I was a single parent doing my best to start over with three young children. I knew I couldn't do it well alone, but I didn't realize exactly what that meant. Tate, my seven-year-old son, made it very clear that he was yearning for a mom two months after losing Kaci, especially when he asked, "Dad, when are we going to get a new mom?"

That statement blew me away. How could he let go so easily? He knew he had a void and knew exactly what he needed to fill it—even at his young age. He asked this question only days before Jess reached out to me with a comment on my blog for the first time. I had prayed for guidance and was confused when what seemed to be an answer arrived so quickly. To be honest, I questioned God at that moment. For months, I had pleaded with him to heal Kaci and was met with nothing but silence, and now, it was just days and maybe even hours after I prayed a simple prayer: *God, I don't know what to do next or how to move forward. Please make it clear!* And then Jess wrote me. It was his answer, and it seemed too quick! What was he thinking?

But God had a plan, and now it was time to let him lead. I did, hesitantly at first, but then I felt a freedom I hadn't experienced in a long time as I began writing Jess. I felt love for another woman, and with that feeling came guilt. I didn't trust God wholeheartedly and felt like I was breaking a vow that I had already fulfilled. Jess is right: it's *'til death do us part*. But, at first, I still felt guilty, and I brought baggage into our marriage. I deeply regret this now—this inability to face my grief before moving on—but I'm thankful I trusted God enough to push forward in spite of my shortcomings. I don't recommend the way we did everything, but when I walked the path God laid out, the result was a blessing tied to obedience. I often strayed, but I kept moving forward.

Grieving is necessary and, unfortunately, I didn't face anything until after Jess and I were married. I used our newfound love to distract me and fill a void—as many widowers do with unsuspecting women. It was unfair and made our relationship more difficult, but it didn't change the fact that I truly loved Jess. When we were first married, I hadn't released all the active marital love I had previously for Kaci, but as I grieved and grew closer to Jess, I realized she deserved more. I can't say exactly when this moment occurred, but today Jess has 100 percent of my spousal love, as I believe it should be in any healthy marriage; however, if I had worked through some of this prior to remarriage, I could have given her my whole heart on our wedding day—like she deserved.

My recommendation? Don't remarry if you're not ready to give your new spouse 100 percent. It's not fair. This is a boundary that you should be uncompromising about as you move forward in a new relationship—your lack of commitment will only cause comparisons, insecurities, and undue pain.

Size-Two Capris: Comparisons and Insecurities

Funny story—or not so funny. During our short dating period and into our first year of marriage, Ryan and I incessantly talked about our late spouses, making comparisons, celebrating newfound freedoms, and mourning what we had lost. We were working through our grief, whether we understood this or not, as we examined the thoughts and patterns of our previous lives, magnifying the experiences through the lens of another—consulting, trusting, and offering our hearts through the connection of pain.

What we shared were our recent experiences with another person, having not been together long enough to solidify a common past with one another. If we had dated other individuals or had even taken a break from being in a relationship, some of the need to discuss our former lives would have dissipated, but because there was very little time between the passing of our spouses and our relationship, the wounds and memories were fresh, and we unloaded. It was awkward at times. There were tears. It was messy and joyful and therapeutic as we pored over what we had gained and expressed sorrow over what was lost. It was a twisty, messed-up, crazy experience to fall in love while grieving the lost love of another. Although there were occasionally healthy conversations, usually our words crossed boundaries as insecurities and doubts surfaced and comparisons, spoken and unspoken, began to take shape.

The problem with comparing yourself to anyone is that it's often not completely accurate. There's no way to understand the entire context, and in a remarriage, we often aren't privy to the bigger picture of a previous marriage based on just a few conversations. In our situation, there was no way we could compare ourselves to the whole truth—we weren't there! And I believe this principle should be applied to most relationships—when dealing with a friendship, a divorce, or memories of a late spouse.

Never speak ill of the dead is a common cliché, and if the theory is subscribed to in real life, it can become detrimental to the emotional well-being of the new spouse. The living are plagued with numerous shortcomings and irritating personality traits—traits that are fully acknowledged and complained about by those who love them—whereas a deceased loved one is often sainted, with shortcomings forgotten the moment they breathed their last, only remembered for the good they contributed to the world. We know instinctively that no human being goes through life in a state of constant perfection, but we have a difficult time owning this truth when somebody dies.

Ryan and I avoided speaking about only the positive qualities of our late spouses and instead spoke freely about everything related to our previous marriages—good, bad, and mediocre. It was a way for us to work through our grief, but these seemingly harmless conversations often backfired, and the comparison game sometimes reared its ugly head.

Jason was a personal trainer, tennis professional, and gym owner. Ryan didn't work out. When I first spoke with him on the phone, he informed me that he was a great tennis player—on the Wii. He later informed me that Jason's preoccupation with health and fitness initially made things a bit difficult for him. Reminders about Jason's fitness and health consciousness seemingly popped up everywhere: from exercise equipment, to fitness T-shirts that Caleb and I wore, to Jason's gym memorabilia, to numerous photos of Jason flexing his six-pack.

One of my big insecurities was tied to how much smaller Kaci was than me. She was a petite girl from the South. I am not. I'm a tall, big-boned Dutch girl from Michigan. She fit nicely under the cup of Ryan's armpit, with his 5'11" stature. I didn't and often had to slouch to shimmy under his shoulder.

One summer morning, we decided to tackle some of the excess baggage in our life and sorted through numerous bags of Kaci and Jason's belongings. In the process of rummaging, Ryan innocently mentioned, "If there's anything you want to keep, go ahead."

It was kind of weird, and honestly, I couldn't even imagine fitting into her clothes. I replied that I would consider anything with the sales tags still attached. This seemed like a good compromise. The tags represented that she hadn't totally committed to the item or else it would have been worn. At the end of the day, I had a small pile of items to consider—one of which was a pair of size-two white capri shorts. I was still painfully thin from the grieving period I had been through and generally wore a size six, but I was optimistic on this particular day, and these shorts appeared to run bigger than a size two. They were cute. They still had the tags attached. Worth a shot, right? But when I tried them on, I couldn't even shimmy one leg halfway up my thigh. And then I knew. I now had a visual representation of how different we were in size, and I thought, *I wonder what Ryan thinks about how much bigger I am than she was?*

I put the shorts in the Goodwill pile, and then I worked myself into an emotional tizzy over how much larger I was compared to his late wife was and how disgusted he was going to be when I started to put the weight back on that I had lost while mourning Jason's death. This same insecurity would flare in the heat of battle—when we were arguing about absolutely nothing having to do with my size or her size. I look back in hindsight and can see the ridiculousness, but at the time, I wasn't completely trusting Ryan's love for me and me alone. That's what comparisons do in the long run. They strip away your God-given beauty and replace it with insecurity. I was never meant to be her, and she was never meant to be me.

Those early conversations, relating our experiences back to ones with our late spouses, were laid to rest as we slowly made memories together and could then reflect more objectively on the security of our relationship and love for one another.

Our journey to peace has been a low and slow process, sometimes with the red-hot flames of passion and other times with red-hot flames of anger, but always simply satisfying as we come to a resolution through open communication and honesty—kind of like this spaghetti sauce, which is an all-time family favorite and pairs well with any pasta dish.

- 3–4 tbsp olive oil
- 1 large onion, chopped
- 4 garlic cloves, chopped
- Add 2 28-ounce cans of quality tomatoes (crushed or whole is fine—I like Carmelina brand)

- Fresh spinach, chopped
- 4 tbsp Italian seasoning
- 2–4 tbsp sugar or maple syrup (depending on how sweet your taste buds are)
- ¼ cup red wine
- 2–3 tbsp tomato paste for a thicker sauce
- Salt and pepper to taste

Sauté the onion and garlic with the olive oil. Add the rest of the ingredients and simmer on low for an hour or two, stirring occasionally. Turn the heat off and blend together with a hand mixer. This recipe gets even tastier after a day or two. The flavors come together, low and slow, and the sauce provides the perfect accompaniment for a pasta dish, for a lasagna, or just for dipping crusty garlic bread into.

(If you're enjoying these recipes, you can find them all available for print on my website: www.jessplusthemess.com/blendedrecipes.)

Take a Number: Constructing Healthy and Loving Boundaries with Your New Family

This is as sensitive as it gets with topics related to blended households: the extended family. It's the family who lost a son or a daughter, the family who loved their child's spouse, the family who is really struggling with how quickly their child's spouse is moving on with a new love, the family who wipes away tears every time they visit as they gaze upon their grandchildren. The feelings, the emotions, the angst, the pain—as delicate as glass those first couple of years.

Ryan and I didn't set out to hurt anyone, but by falling in love, we seemed to entirely fail at this mission. When we became a family, there were twenty-two grandparents. Yep. You read that correctly. Between our blended families, great-grandparents, and the extended family of the late spouses, we were surrounded by a multitude, and each family member seemed to have an opinion about our new life together. We quickly became dream slashers when expectations were presented by those around us, and the saying *take a number* became an ongoing joke after delivering disappointing news time and again when we couldn't or wouldn't jump through hoops to make someone's desire a reality. It was exhausting and overwhelming to feel like we were constantly letting everyone down and to have to explain ourselves when we did participate in an activity which then led to hurt feelings from other family members. We often chose to slither away from everything and everyone to avoid hurtful confrontations.

When the dust finally settled, we had to identify how we were going to parent our seven children and operate our household. The majority of what had worked in our previous lives with smaller families was not going to work in a new reality. Ryan's life was much more carefree with his three healthy children, and he had to adapt to the unique challenges our son Lucas, who has special needs, presented in our life. We both had a lot to figure out about this larger family structure, and our lessons began with incorporating boundaries, with the first boundary involving our guest policy.

When Ryan was a child, his family often welcomed out-of-town guests into their home. They didn't have a spare bedroom, but people would bring their sleeping bags and sprawl out in the family room, wherever they found space. Ryan and Kaci continued this tradition and would welcome people into their home on a consistent basis. Growing up in my big family, we *never* had anyone spend the night in our home. Never. Ever. There were a couple of reasons for this. First, we already had twelve individuals under one roof and space was limited, and second, people weren't vying to spend the night at the Bossenbroeks, with their herd of kids. Finally, most of our immediate family lived in town, so there wasn't a reason to accommodate out-of-town guests. Jason and I also never had overnight visitors—again, a different history. We had Lucas, who didn't sleep for years; I was popping out babies every other year; and Jason fought cancer for three years. We most likely were not the first family people thought of when considering their overnight options.

Ryan and I started our relationship with different expectations for out-of-town guests because we entered our life together with a different set of histories. His philosophy was *the more the merrier!* Mine was *we already have nine people in this house, and I don't think my introverted, emotionally unstable self can handle entertaining on top of the chaos that seven children and special needs and grief and a blended home brings*. But—I sucked it up and didn't say anything as out-of-towners rotated in and out of my house on a bimonthly basis that first year.

This frustration worked in reverse as well. When we visited extended family out of state, I wanted my space and didn't want to stay in others' homes. I grew up this way. We never stayed in someone's house when we traveled and instead opted for a hotel, or we took our travel trailer to keep costs down. I own my strange ways, and I'm admittedly an old soul. I like familiar routines and rhythms, and these became highly important to my mental well-being with seven kids in tow.

In our first home together, we set aside a guest room per Ryan's coaxing. I thought I'd give it a try and became immediately overwhelmed as my type-A perfectionist personality sought to cook three gourmet meals a day and keep the house clean, lest my new family think I was failing at this life I had chosen. The pressure mounted to put my best foot forward as the "new mom" in front of my new family. I did not—above anything—want to appear incompetent, and so I put on a brave face and smiled and entertained and cleaned and cooked to the best of my ability, and at the end of the day, as my husband sat on the couch chatting away with our guests, I said goodnight to the kids and snuck away, where I enjoyed a long, hot, peaceful bath while the tears fell swiftly down my face. I was overwhelmed and didn't know how to share these emotions with my husband. In my mind, he had moved to Michigan for me, for my kids, leaving his whole family behind in Oklahoma, and the least I could do was entertain our guests when they visited.

We never had a blow-out argument or tense conversations because I felt strongly that it was my duty to suck it up, and I did. We continued this way for about a year, and then in a very passive-aggressive attempt to change what wasn't apparently working for either of us, we began to consider moving. Far away. Somewhere in the middle of nowhere to stake out a life for our family. All by ourselves. Not in Michigan and not in Oklahoma. We began our search in 2013 and landed in Bath Springs, Tennessee—two years after we said *I do*. We uprooted our family of nine and moved because, I believe, we were both desperate for breathing room, but neither of us knew how to approach the subject or get what we needed without hurting more people. Instead, we did what any rational, mature human being would do—we moved our family from civilization to somewhere quiet. Really quiet—where the nearest mall was more than an hour away. And we found peace, at least for a while. And once we were in this new land of ours, we bought a small cottage—for out-of-town guests—and that was a *victory*, as I was now a mom to eight children (including a newborn baby). Oh, and our solution for our family vacations included the purchase of a travel trailer that slept ten! Yep, we got a great deal, and it has provided loads of family fun, along with peace and routine for this introverted momma.

A happy marriage starts with healthy boundaries—although I'm not sure running away to the middle of rural Tennessee is the best way to approach a problem. But it did relieve our angst temporarily. Maybe you don't have to take such a drastic approach and can have the hard conversation that we avoided. I would suggest going that route, if possible. However you instill those hedges of protection around your new family, understand that it is okay to request space as you figure out your life together. You won't need a huge expanse forever, but you do need grace during the first two or three years as you lay a foundation. Next up, we'll discuss why making dedicated time for the new marriage is necessary for a successful family, and we'll explore a few tried-and-true methods that have helped us prioritize our relationship in the midst of chaos.

When I think of healthy anything, I usually think of a way to make a favorite dish a little more nutrient friendly, like this one—healthy cornbread. It could be entirely gluten- and dairy-free if you choose. Enjoy!

- ¼ cup melted butter or ghee (or plant-based butter for a dairy-free option)
- ¼ cup melted coconut oil
- ½ cup plus 2 tbsp maple syrup
- 2 eggs
- ½ tsp baking soda
- ¾ cup almond milk
- 1 cup flour (or almond flour for a gluten-free option)
- 1 cup cornmeal
- ½ tsp salt

Mix the butter and coconut oil together in a big bowl. Add the maple syrup to the butter/oil mixture. Stir well. Cool this mixture. Add the rest of the ingredients. Mix well. Grease a large cast-iron skillet with coconut oil. Pour mixture into the skillet and bake at 375 degrees for 20 minutes.

3

THE GIFT OF A HAPPY MARRIAGE

Laying a *Firm* Foundation

Ryan and I married quickly—some would say too quickly—but we considered several variables during our decision. We met in late 2010, got engaged in January 2011, and were married by April. In this short dating window, we wrote daily emails, sent constant texts, talked on the phone for hours, flew back and forth between Michigan and Oklahoma, sometimes met in between, and read everything the other had written on their blog. We packed years of information into a few months. Additionally, we were both committed to the concept of marriage, our faith, and our children, and had shown this deep commitment through many of the darkest days in our previous relationships. If a marriage can weather brain cancer, a child with profound special needs, and near poverty, it can handle the complexities that a new relationship with seven children would bring. I preface all this to ultimately say, when Ryan and I vowed to love, honor, and cherish one another 'til death do us part, we knew our relationship had to be a number-one priority or we would fail ourselves and our children in numerous ways. We were newlyweds who hadn't had many opportunities to date face to face, and there were still abundant mysteries to uncover about our personalities, ways of navigating through the world, and how we viewed life in general. Although we were deeply in love and attracted to one another, we realized that passionate endorphins don't last forever. We understood that in order to give our children the gift of a long-term marriage, we would have to make our time together a priority, and this wouldn't happen without intentional planning. We diligently set aside time to communicate, bond, and have fun together; however, this was difficult to accomplish with seven grieving children who also required our limited time. We devised a well-thought-out plan that allowed us to be present for the kids but also gave us alone time to cultivate a healthy, lasting relationship. This plan involved two daily policies. One of these policies was a commitment to pray together every morning, and the second became the eight o'clock rule.

The first policy is simple. We pray together every morning. It takes all of ten minutes and can be constructed to fit numerous schedule restraints if something unexpected arises. Annabelle, our youngest, has been crawling on and off our laps during these sessions throughout the past few years, and although it is a distraction, it's our annoyance—not the Lord's. On the rare occasion that busyness gets the better of our morning, or we forget or can't be together physically, we've incorporated text prayers, which start the day on a high note of continued commitment to our faith and marriage. This tradition sets a positive precedence for our relationship and has eliminated the growth of resentment or hurt feelings because we are scheduled to bring our problems to a higher power within a twenty-four-hour period.

The second daily policy is the eight o'clock rule, which is just as it sounds—everyone remove yourself from the common areas of the home and retreat to your bedroom at 8:00 p.m. (so Mom and Dad can have some alone time). This rule has loosened as the kids age, but the premise remains the same. As a family, we gather at 7:30 to pray, and then the kids leave us alone from eight o'clock onward. The big boys have a basement bedroom, so they have more flexibility than the other kids to play video games, watch movies, or read books. The rest read books or draw or watch a movie, and Ryan and I resort to our bedroom to spend quality time together. I recently read *Bringing Up Bébé* by Pamela Druckerman and discovered that this strict bedtime structure is a commonality throughout France. French parents highly value and prioritize time as a couple, and most incorporate something similar with their children. Who knew the Ronnes were so culturally chic?

Ryan's Take

The eight o'clock rule has been great for us and shows our children that our marriage is a top priority. I know many question how it's possible to get our kids to comply, but it's simple. We tell them it's wind-down time, and they typically listen. If they don't, consequences will ensue. They know we love them and want to spend time with them—just not at eight o'clock at night.

Another high priority in our busy life is a weekly date night, and we rarely miss this. It's not always easy, but it is important to get away—even for a couple of hours. Occasionally, circumstances don't allow us to leave the house, and then we have to get creative. We feed the kids, send them downstairs or outside, and sit down together to have a nice, quiet dinner. At least that's the plan. Typically, we get about five minutes before someone starts to cry, Annabelle sneaks away from whoever is watching her, or one of our dear ones has a question that must be answered or the world may end. This time together is so important that even when Jess was eight months pregnant, we still went out for dinner, and after Annabelle was born, she accompanied us until she was old enough to stay home with a sitter. We usually go out on a Saturday, and before we can leave, Jess prepares food for the kids, and I feed and bathe Lucas and put a movie on so that he's occupied for a while. When we finally head out, we exhale deeply as the stress is lifted. For the next two hours, we are free from bickering, crying, dirty diapers, teenage eye rolls, and the never-ending tasks of our chaotic life.

We also try to get away for a weekend a few times a year to refresh and regroup. These getaways are usually simple. We rent a hotel room for a couple of nights, eat good food, listen to music, and sleep as long as our bodies will allow. We do our best to plan a more elaborate trip once a year or every other year that gives us a bit of a sabbatical. We don't do amusement parks or high-intensity adventures; we go somewhere to simply relax. I'll admit, I'm much better at this concept than Jess is, but there is something about these longer trips that helps her feel the freedom to unwind. We walk a lot, eat lots of food (which is why we walk a lot), stay up a little later, and sleep in every morning. We don't typically plan our day until we roll out of bed, have a few cups of coffee, and see how we feel. These trips give us a chance to rest and reflect, and they remind us of how fortunate we are and how much we really do enjoy the life we have.

In my previous marriage, I wasn't good at this. I didn't understand the importance of prioritizing marriage and often got dragged around on adventures and occasional dates, never fully participating. I have been given a second chance, and I benefit greatly from it. I will admit, there is always room for improvement, but I make the effort now. I have a beautiful wife, and I want to enjoy her company.

How can you send the message to your spouse that he or she is a top priority? Maybe it's a cup of coffee together in the morning. Maybe it's meeting for a quick lunch at the park. Maybe it's planning a date in the deer stand for a quickie—southern humor here—or perhaps it's spending a few hours at your favorite restaurant. Whatever it is, make it happen. Those moments of reconnecting with your spouse and enjoying one another are the best gift you can give your children.

One of our favorite stuck-at-home date-night meals is this simple chicken dish, marinated in honey mustard and a dash of paprika with a slice of bacon and white cheddar cheese melted on top. We often pair this with a kale Caesar salad and dark chocolate mascarpone cheese. The whole bit takes about twenty minutes to prep—really.

- 2 chicken breasts
- 1 cup honey
- 1 cup Dijon mustard
- Dash of paprika
- Salt and pepper to taste
- 2 slices of precooked bacon
- 2 slices of cheddar cheese

Wisk together the first three ingredients. Generously prick the chicken with a fork, salt and pepper both sides, and cover with the marinade either in a plastic bag or a baking dish. Marinate for a few hours in the fridge—the longer, the better. We often cook ours on the grill, but a cast-iron skillet works too. When the chicken is cooked through, top with the bacon and cheese. Cover until melted.

Kale Caesar Salad

I discovered this salad at the Austin airport of all weird places, and it quickly became a favorite, healthy(ish) spin on one of my indulgences.

- Bag of prewashed, precut kale (because we're all about easy)
- Parmesan cheese (or nutritional yeast for a dairy-free option)
- Your favorite Caesar dressing
- Your favorite croutons (or ground almonds for a gluten-free option)

Toss the ingredients together, except for the croutons, and let the flavors come together in the fridge for an hour or two. Add the croutons or almonds just before serving.

Dark Chocolate Mascarpone Cheese

We also enjoy this easy dessert option, which only has two ingredients and comes together nicely after a few hours in the fridge.

- 8 ounces of mascarpone cheese
- 2 cups of dark chocolate chips

Melt on a stove top in a double boiler over low heat. Pour into ramekins. Refrigerate for a few hours until solid.

Josh and Jada: How Two of Our Kids Taught Us to Prioritize Friendship

Josh and Jada. Jada and Josh. These two don't remember life without the other. They met for the first time in March 2011 when Jada was one and Josh was eighteen months old. Ryan brought his crew to my house, where we ate pizza and connected before the wedding. Josh and Jada were outside on the deck. Josh had never been around people his size before, and he became a bit excited. Jada was standing at the top of the stairs, and Josh reached out and pushed her. She fell down the stairs. And sobbed. And sobbed and sobbed and sobbed, and when she stood up, she had one less tooth. Fortunately for Josh, all was quickly forgiven, and these two became the best of friends. As the other kids ventured off to school, they played together, all day, every day. They were curious. They had fun. They were brave.

I was home one beautiful summer day with my then two-year-olds while Ryan made improvements on my previous house in preparation to sell it. I kept my eye on our two youngest while cleaning the kitchen and suddenly realized the house was eerily quiet. I began calling out, "Josh! Jada!"

My calm yells quickly turned to frantic outbursts as I scoured every square inch of the house and was unable to locate them; however, I did discover an open door in the basement. They had been quietly playing, and apparently that play had turned to boredom. I ran outside, yelling, "Josh! Jada! Where are you?!"

I checked behind bushes, in the barn, in the woods, and along the side of our house. Nothing. They were nowhere to be seen. I was convinced Ryan would leave me when he discovered what an incompetent mother I was, and by now, the tears were streaming. I stared straight up our long dirt driveway, which led to a long dusty road and into our development (with a total of three houses), which led to a major street at the end of it all.

I began to run, yelling with every pounding footstep, "Josh! Jada!"

I ran past the mailbox and over a slight hill that had limited my view. I ran and ran and ran and then—there they were. Josh and Jada. Walking along the side of the road, in the grass, hand in hand. And there was my husband, in his truck, smiling at the two of them.

"Honey!" I sobbed as I came upon the scene, panting and panicked, "Honey, I'm sorry! They escaped from the basement when I wasn't looking. I'm so sorry!"

He smiled, almost amused at the situation, apparently not planning on leaving me.

"Mistakes happen. They're fine!"

And they were fine. As fine as two friends could be. Walking hand in hand like big hotshots, knowing enough to stay off the road! But, boy, did I keep a much more diligent eye on them from that day forward!

Josh and Jada's friendship makes me think of my own friendship with Ryan. Not only did we quickly build a connection and fall in love, but we've always had a foundation of fun at the core of our relationship. We laugh a lot, and a good hearty laugh can be hard to come by with me! I don't tend to find things all that funny, but Ryan has a redneck comedic bit that gets me rolling with laughter. I'm convinced he'll be seen on a comedy circuit one day. But that's really what it's about in a good marriage—cultivating those times together, laughing, listening, and holding each other's hand as you walk down the dusty path of life.

Ryan and I have learned a few valuable lessons about marriage from observing Josh and Jada's relationship. Many of these lessons include random acts of kindness—which goes a long way in any marriage. Why do we so often forget to be kind to the one person we say we love more than anyone else in the world? One afternoon, Jada was really struggling to get her shoes on and Josh took charge: "Jada, you sit down, and I'll put your shoe on your foot."

Jada obediently sat down and accepted his help. She didn't berate him with comments about how she could do it herself. She simply accepted his help. Or there was another incident when they were screaming at each other and Jada yelled, "I'm never playing with you again!" Josh stormed off, but about ten minutes later, he decided to check in on his female counterpart. Sure enough, they resumed playing as if nothing had happened. Men, hear this truth, we love it when you overlook our emotional outbursts and come back pretending like nothing happened, and this reaction is probably in your best interest if you don't want a marathon gab session.

One of my favorite memories involves Josh and Jada when they were four years old. They were instructed to clean up a big mess before they could take out another toy. This mess consisted of about five billion little Matchbox cars scattered all over the living room floor, and they needed to be put away in the toybox after being gathered up in a laundry basket. These two worked together—one pushing, the other pulling—until they were able to get this basket back to the toy closet, where Jada then struggled to put it on the shelf. She asked Josh if he could help her. He agreed, and as he huffed and puffed and flexed his little muscles, she proudly declared, "Josh, you're *so* strong!" Josh beamed upon hearing this.

Ryan laughed and said jokingly, "It's that simple. Tell a man he's strong, and we'll do whatever you want."

This advice came in handy one afternoon when I almost burned our homestead down in an attempt to be helpful.

That Time I Almost Burned the House Down: Prioritizing Teamwork in a Marriage

I loved our rural Tennessee life after we moved from Michigan. I loved the garden and the chickens and hanging freshly laundered linens on the line. I loved the raw, natural essence, as we relied on one another to meet our basic needs. I loved our creativity when things didn't go as planned, such as using our oil lamps when the power went out—yet again. I loved hearing the kids suggest we fry up the crickets they caught and then laughing when they said they tasted like popcorn. We caught catfish in the river and hiked through the woods like we were Davy Crockett and his band of men. We slept under the stars. We took advantage of the beauty and the thirty acres of timber that surrounded our house on the hill. Ryan and I were determined to learn everything we could about homesteading, and we intended to be as self-sufficient as possible. He chopped firewood. We planted a vineyard, fruit trees, and vegetables, and raised chickens for meat and eggs. However, what I didn't expect with our move to rural America was that there wouldn't be any trash service. This confused me. My whole life, wherever I had lived—in the whole big state of Michigan—we had been able to locate a trash service company, but here, this was not offered. Instead, there were trash centers, and it was the homeowner's responsibility to take the trash to these locations. Ryan and I eventually decided this was a positive practice in the world of homesteading, because not only would we save money but we would be more mindful about our wastefulness.

We made it a point to deliver our trash once a week, but with a large family, that meant we were going to live with a heap of rubbish the remaining six days. Our solution was to collect any cardboard boxes, paper, or flammable materials in a separate bin and then burn these contents in the firepit every couple of days.

While the kids were at school one day, I was puttering about in my kitchen and Ryan was renovating the cottage we had purchased for guests. I noticed that the burn bin was overflowing with boxes and paper. I had never actually burned the contents in this bin before, but I was feeling ambitious and decided this mess needed to be discarded immediately. I thought Ryan would appreciate having one of his responsibilities accomplished by his loving wife.

I hauled the overflowing bin out to the ledge of the cliff, where our firepit overlooked a huge expanse of trees. I took a few of the newspapers and placed them at the bottom of the pit, stacked a handful of twigs on top to keep them in place, and lit a match. It was then, as the flame was immediately snuffed out, that I noticed the wind. Ignorance clouded common sense, and it didn't compute that this wasn't the best idea on an extremely windy day. I lit the match again and sheltered the tiny flickering flame with cardboard. The flame came alive. I threw more paper and cardboard on top, and the flame swayed back and forth, growing larger and building in momentum as it danced in sync with the wind. Satisfied with the progress of my fire, I ran into the house to switch the laundry to the clothesline on our deck. I opened the door with laundry in hand and stepped outside, only to gasp in disbelief. Around the firepit and down the steep ledge were mini fires, dancing in the wind and growing in strength by the minute. The paper had not remained in the pit as I had imagined it would have and instead had been carried away by the gusts of wind into the surrounding areas.

"Oh crap!"

I ran to survey the damage. I was shocked and didn't have any idea how I would perform damage control on this mess, terrified that my house was about to go up in flames if I didn't get a handle on the problem!

"Crap, Crap, Crap!" along with some other choice words, escaped my frantic lips.

I quickly retrieved as many buckets and empty paint containers as I could hold. Running back and forth to the spicket, I made slow and steady progress, but as I put out the bigger fires, the smaller ones continued to gain momentum, finding nearby debris or leaves to stoke their little fire hearts. My mind was racing.

Should I call the fire department? Call Ryan? Resolve this problem on my own? This last thought is my go-to tendency, as I hate to admit that I need help, but this was quickly erupting out of my control. I needed my husband.

I picked up the phone and punched in his number. He answered immediately.

"Honey," I gasped. "I need you to come home immediately! The yard's on fire!"

Thankfully he didn't ask any questions and took my word for it. He quickly arrived, looked around at the dire situation, and asked, "What happened?!"

"I decided to burn the paper, but I didn't realize it would blow all over the yard!" I blurted out.

"Okay, keep getting buckets of water," he instructed.

The two of us set to work, side by side, filling buckets. I realized how scary the situation was when Ryan didn't blow it off, as he so often does. This apparently was a big deal. We worked together for over an hour, lugging buckets of water to the numerous fires and extinguishing them one by one. Finally, there were no more flickering hot lights, and our property was safe. I was emotionally and physically exhausted, and fell into my husband's helpful arms.

As I attempted to catch my breath, a favorite verse came to mind: "Two are better than one, because they have a good return for their labor: If either of them falls down, one can help the other up" (Eccles. 4:9–10).

Ryan and I sure had a good return on our ability to work together that day. Our labor saved our homestead from potential ruin! Teamwork makes the dream work—so they say, unless we're talking about football. But that's a different story altogether . . .

Football and Brisket Sandwiches: Prioritizing Communication for a Healthy Relationship

Football. The word elicits images of my husband zoned out on the couch as he watches a group of men in tight pants run up and down a field. I don't understand the appeal. The whole premise of the game suggests an untapped, primal urge in many men that needs exploring. Perhaps a concept of manhood that was left underdeveloped in their childhood. There is a moral to this story—I promise.

I was not raised around football. I can't recall my father ever voluntarily watching a game. My only memories of the sport include a specific Thanksgiving celebration when my uncle turned the television on after dinner—not prior to the meal or during but after. The Thanksgiving meal was viewed as a sacred time to reflect on family, faith, and thankfulness—not football. My four brothers, to my knowledge, don't play the game or watch it religiously, and my late husband Jason didn't care for it either.

During our first years together, Ryan assumed that lazy Sunday afternoons were made specifically for us to watch his favorite game. The first year I indulged this desire, and he indulged my desire to cuddle while watching. It was a win-win. We lived in Michigan and had delivery options at our disposal, and if I didn't want to cook dinner, we ordered pizza at halftime. I was deeply in love with my new husband and was perfectly content to cuddle as we watched almost anything of his choosing. All that changed when we weren't newlyweds anymore and moved to rural Tennessee.

First, although I'm still deeply in love with my husband, those raging endorphins from the good ole days that would have allowed him to watch, say, or do anything have diminished significantly. Also, there were zero delivery options in our new hometown in Tennessee. I came to resent having to scramble to prepare a meal while Ryan blissfully zoned out, watching football. Part of the problem was internal, as I struggled to relax and instead used the Sabbath to cook, clean, and get caught up on laundry. Part of the problem involved a few tasks we couldn't eliminate from our schedules—even on a Sunday—because they were directly tied to caring for children. Lucas and Annabelle needed to be fed, bathed, and diapered. These were nonnegotiable tasks. I resented football because Ryan was so relaxed that he often required friendly reminders to attend to these vital tasks, and I didn't enjoy reminding a grown man of his responsibilities.

Ryan's Take

First off, here's a little of my background. I played football at a young age and was actually pretty good at it. I was in a lot of pain emotionally as a child, and football encouraged me to take out my frustrations. It was therapy. As I became older, I realized I wasn't built for football, and although I had the heart of a linebacker, I was small. I would run full speed and hit whoever had the ball as hard as I could, which only resulted in me being on the ground. My coaches would praise me, "Nice hit" or "That kid's got heart," and then under their breath mutter, "Too bad he's so small." In my freshman year of high school, I had a defining moment. I was playing defense, jumped up to block a pass, and came down on another player's knee, cracking several of my ribs. I had never felt pain like that, and at 5'2" and 100 pounds, I wisely walked away from contact sports.

When my dad was around, he and I would watch football together—even if he was annoyed by my constant questions. I remember going to church with my mom and sister on Sunday morning, and when we returned home, we would find my dad in his recliner with a game on. I didn't think of it as him choosing football over us, but I did wonder what I was missing if he would skip church for it.

Football was also a big deal at Thanksgiving dinners, as it is for most normal people. (Sorry, babe!) Part of this tradition came from my South Dakota family, who were mostly Minnesota Vikings fans. Living in Oklahoma, the television stations rarely aired a Vikings game, except on Thanksgiving Day. During my first marriage, I arrived at my new in-laws' house for what I thought would be a traditional Thanksgiving holiday (with football), and to my chagrin, the Macy's Day parade was on the television. The explanation? "We don't watch football on Thanksgiving—we talk." Another guest and I snuck downstairs to watch the game.

Today football has a different meaning. It's a way for me to relax as I watch two teams of disciplined, fit, and athletic men strategizing in a game that is full of excitement. I honestly don't understand how you couldn't want to watch it! I understand that my family deserves a portion of my limited free time, but I also need to relax to be the best version of myself. Honestly, I do check out when there is a game on because I'm not like my wife—I don't multitask well.

Through the years, we've learned how to communicate and compromise about this issue, and Jess has learned the difference between being reactive and reflective. I've learned to say what I'm thinking, even if it will ruffle her feathers a bit—like what happened recently when I said, "Hey honey, I'd like to watch two games on Sunday. I'm letting you know ahead of time."

Silence. I hope she's reflecting.

Like a brave soldier, I continue: "I know you want help on Sundays, so what do you want me to be aware of?"

Typically, there is a negotiation process. She may ask me to finish a task that morning or check on Lucas during commercials, and then I try to remember the ways she needs help. As long as I don't totally check out, she will limit her sarcastic remarks about men running around in tights.

A few other compromises that work well include a discussion beforehand about how many games will be watched on a specific weekend. I don't like surprises and handle circumstances much better if I can mentally prepare for what's ahead.

I'm starting to understand how men typically operate in a linear way and thrive when focused on one task at a time. Women are often all over the map and have numerous thoughts floating about at one time. Now I know that Ryan is happy to help; it simply isn't on his radar as he is focused on the task at hand—watching football.

We have also made room in the budget to occasionally enlist help for Lucas so that we can both truly relax.

Football was obviously not the primary issue in this situation, but it triggered feelings that ultimately led to other bigger issues. What's your trigger? Maybe it's when the in-laws come to visit. Or when your adopted child screams, "You're not my real dad!" Or maybe it's picking up your husband's dirty socks off the floor. Whatever it is, try getting ahead of the game and talk to your spouse before you wind up tackling each other with words. Outline in detail what your expectations are to avoid unsportsmanlike calls in the future.

To solve the *What are we going to eat?* dilemma, I'll often put a brisket in the oven Saturday evening and let it cook on low all night. The pull-apart meat melts in your mouth and is used for brisket sandwiches or nachos the next day. Yum! It's so good, and it makes the house smell amazing. Here is a recipe for our go-to game-day sandwiches. Heck, if I'm going to be watching a four-hour marathon of men running around in tights, I want tasty food to snack on. I'd love to know your go-to easy football snacks. Chime in on social media (@jessplusthemess), and I'll compile a list for all of us women stuck in the football trenches.

- 10–15 pounds brisket
- 1 7-ounce can of chipotle peppers in adobe sauce
- ¼ cup apple cider vinegar
- ½–1 cup broth (vegetable, bone, or beef)
- Salt and pepper to taste

Generously salt and pepper the brisket. Add the peppers, vinegar, and broth. Put in the oven at 200 degrees before going to bed. Let it cook all night long. In the morning, check on the progress. Depending on when you'll be eating it (lunch or dinner), turn up the heat to around 300/350 degrees if it's still too tough to shred with a fork and continue watching it throughout the day. It's done when it easily shreds. Let it marinate in the sauce for 30–60 minutes. Potato salad or coleslaw make nice sides. Use the leftover meat for brisket nachos topped with cheese and pickled jalapenos.

4

THE GOOD FEELINGS HAVE LEFT THE BUILDING

Learning to *Cope* When Marriage Is *Hard*

The seven-year itch is a thing—because it seems to be true. Marriages reach this mythical seven-year marker, and the relationship often becomes difficult. The endorphins fade as exhaustion sets in and raising children takes center stage—in our case, teens, toddlers, special needs, and everything in between—and there's the more than occasional doubting thought. *Is this really my life?!*

Our overwhelming life has elicited an occasional conversation—words barely whispered. *Is the exhaustion worth it? How do we continue?*

We've questioned a life we were once eager to begin but lately felt like we were in over our heads, with sleep deprivation and numerous responsibilities. Instead of looking at one another with warmth and understanding, glares of contempt seared across the room and bickering replaced dreams and hand holding on date night. A time or two (or three), I have questioned many blessings in my life and have threatened to destroy it all if people don't get in line and bend to my will. Pretty picture, huh?

A particular argument began one cloudy afternoon in March 2018, the seven-year marker in our marriage, a year saturated with petty bitterness as we sought to accommodate our family's needs in rural Tennessee—needs that felt increasingly burdensome as Lucas aged and started puberty. The argument began, as they so often did, over an unmet expectation (about putting groceries away) and then unraveled into a mud-slinging event as sharp words pierced the air.

"You brought the groceries into the house and then just left them on the counter for me to put away?" I asked

"That's how we always do it!" Ryan hissed in reply.

"Maybe that's how we do it if the kids are around to help!"

We continued to hurl *never* and *always* statements for the next hour as the piles of groceries lingered on the counter, the ice cream becoming softer by the second as the humid air became thick with disgust. All an extremely productive use of our time while the kids were in school. The insults flew:

"You *never* help with the kids!"

"You *always* nag me about everything!"

"You are *never* someone I can depend on!"

"You *always* need to control *everything*!"

And then we began to discuss every single way either one of us had let the other one down in the past seven years of marriage. These conversations included intensely hurtful reminders that had been forgiven—or should have been—as we dragged each one to the surface and reexamined it in the light of this new, hot anger, which caused havoc and brought pain to our emotional well-being once again.

Yuck.

Eventually, we set aside our pride and put the groceries away—our swift movements blanketed in an eerie silence. With the physical mess remedied, I needed to clear the mental mess in my head, and so I found my walking shoes.

Walking is a way for me to work the angst out of my body, one step at a time, as the stress slowly dissipates with the forward motion. As I put one foot in front of the other, I prayed: *Lord, how do I replace this weariness in my marriage with joy? With peace? How do I change my heart, Lord?*

I trekked up and down the dusty road that made up our never-ending driveway, and I heard a simple response: *Be thankful.*

Really? I questioned. *Could it be that easy?*

I went to the Word, eager to find a verse that would back up what I just heard in my heart, and found this: "Let the peace of Christ rule in your hearts, since as members of one body you were called to peace. And be thankful" (Col. 3:15).

Apparently, it was true. Thankfulness and peace walk hand in hand with one another.

I believed this to be true, but would I act on it? Could I swallow my pride and be thankful for this man the Lord had placed in my life? For all these children? Thankful for Lucas's intense needs? I decided to give it a shot and focus on my blessings.

The next day, I awoke to a surprise. While the Lord was working on changing my crappy attitude to one of gratitude, he was working on Ryan's heart as well. This is what I wrote in a journal entry from 2018.

> My husband's hands gave me three hours of peace today. Three hours I didn't deserve because of the spewing that occurred yesterday. He wrangled the monkey child (Annabelle) and brought her to Lowes, where he purchased carpet for our wooden

steps so that she doesn't wake up early any more with the kids clamoring down at 6:00 a.m. like wild hyenas. His hands graced me with a quiet stillness—a stillness I haven't had in a long time, a stillness I savored. Three hours of peace to remember. To remember gratitude, remember my husband's faithfulness, and remember it's just a moment—a moment I get to choose, and that choice is a gift. A choice of bitterness, anger, and destruction or a choice of love, mercy, and thankfulness. Love won.

TAKEAWAYS

- Change your perspective from bitterness to thankfulness.
- Just keep moving—one foot in front of the other.
- Keep the intimacy alive by doing small acts of kindness for one another, which will light the marriage fires in other places as well.

Mud Pie

This recipe is what I bought the ice cream for that fateful, hot day, and actually it was okay that it melted because it was about to be turned into a childhood favorite of mine and a fan favorite of my crew—a super easy dessert that only improves as the flavors come together in the freezer.

- 1 stick of butter, melted
- 3 cups of Oreos, crushed
- 1 gallon of your favorite ice cream (We like vanilla.)
- A jar of hot fudge

- A jar of caramel
- Whipped cream
- Slivered almonds

Add butter to the cookie crumbs and press the mixture into a 9×13 pan. Freeze the crust for 2–3 hours. Let the ice cream get soft and then add it to the crust. Add the hot fudge and caramel. Top with slivered almonds. Freeze overnight. Cut into slices and add a dollop of whipped cream to each slice.

Help! Admitting You Need Something More

Ryan and I have a joke that I'm the wife who landed him in therapy. Not really all that humorous but true. During our first marriages, we were young and naïve, which led to either a lack of communication or explosive arguments with no resolve—both methods lacking in maturity and discernment. This second time around, I've enforced communication, and he's made it clear that he does not want to engage in explosive (passionate) arguments. Ten years later, I think we're getting the hang of this thing called respect.

While we have managed to communicate through many disagreements, we repeatedly hit an insurmountable impasse when it came to other issues such as trust, and this eventually landed us in a very nice gentleman's office on the east side of Grand Rapids, Michigan. We were pleasantly surprised to learn that many of our problems had very little to do with our relationship, and instead had everything to do with the baggage we brought into the marriage. This baggage from our pasts shaped our perceptions and beliefs regarding the world and the people in it. Since we each had a history that involved loss and abandonment, we both perceived the world and the people in it through a lens of being unsafe. People leave. People die. People reject you. And armed with this series of beliefs, we quickly constructed walls of protection to avoid ever feeling pain like that again. Neither of us had a healthy view of the world due to our baggage, and we were firmly entrenched in protective mode—which can never lead to a loving, trusting, and fulfilling partnership.

The knowledge this kind, older gentleman shared became a stepping stone toward individual healing so that we would be whole enough to partake in a relationship. We had been unintentionally projecting our fears onto each other, and it would require intentional work to rewire our thinking with positivity—work which continues to this day and probably will forever and ever, much to Ryan's dismay.

We haven't stayed in continuous therapy but have recognized the value it plays in certain situations—especially when we feel stuck. We seek it out when we acknowledge that a third-party mediator may be able to offer insights that we're not seeing. Our lack of vision is usually attributed to an emotional attachment we have to the issue. We might not be able to see objectively because a loved one is involved (perhaps ourselves, a child, a family member), or we might have an emotional attachment to a feeling or trade-off we receive by not changing our behavior—a change that may require uncomfortable steps that will lead to growth. Sometimes it seems like the easier option is to entrench our heads deeply in the sand and stay in passive mode. Ignorance is bliss—until it isn't anymore.

We began therapy again after Ryan's struggles with anxiety during the summer of 2017. We were exhausted due to the growing demands of our family, and he began to experience weight loss and have regular panic attacks. This tumultuous period took its toll on our marriage, and we consulted an online therapist (Yes! That's a thing!) because we didn't have the time to attend in-person therapy and the closest real therapist was an hour away.

We learned a lot in a few short weeks. I discovered that I operated from PTSD mode (post-traumatic stress disorder) whenever

Ryan exhibited symptoms of illness because his poor health immediately transported me back with Jason and his plethora of health issues, along with feelings of abandonment and loneliness. When I feel out of control, I become angry, and I use this anger as fuel—the only fuel I can find in the middle of being overwhelmed.

Knowledge is power, and sometimes the retrieval of this knowledge requires another person to bring what you may already be aware of to the surface. I knew that there were other fuel sources available, but I had never explored those options because anger was what I was familiar with. I required a therapist to remind me of alternative refueling options for self-care, such as walking, yoga, and prayer. Her suggestion encouraged me to deliberately choose a healthy fuel and avoid going into full-on panic mode with my angry fuel.

Therapy has had its place in our marriage and has benefited us greatly as we discover more about ourselves and, in turn, incorporate these concepts into being the healthiest "us" possible.

Sometimes therapy is the answer, and sometimes there may be a simpler solution, such as reaching out to a trusted friend. Through the years, I've found that many of my issues stem from feelings of isolation, and it takes a deliberate effort to make sure I'm pursuing community in my busy life.

TAKEAWAYS

- Find a trusted friend or confidant. I often require a good ear who will simply allow me to dump my problems and then offer sound advice without judgment.
- Find authentic community. Despair breeds in isolation.
- Find a book on whatever issue you're dealing with. Therapy can be expensive, and maybe the first stop is the

local bookstore or library, where you might get a better understanding of the problem and possible solutions. How-to books on marriage, blended families, and adoption have been lifesavers as Ryan and I journey through this new life of ours—and have saved us a bunch of money!

- Consider therapy. If you truly need an unbiased individual, find a trusted therapist. We've gone to therapists in person and online. The online option is a far more affordable if money is tight.

Pulling Weeds: Removing Unforgiveness to Experience True Growth and Intimacy

We moved to Tennessee with a dream of living off the land: hunting, fishing, chickens, gardening, and sometimes frying up crickets for a snack. We desired a simple life focused on time together by eliminating many of the distractions of the world. This simplicity included a desire to raise our children with the knowledge of where their food originated from and how it landed on their plates every day.

Ryan had never planted a seed in his life prior to our marriage. I had always cultivated a small garden, and although working the land wasn't something I was necessarily passionate about—it felt more like a chore most of the time—it was an annual pursuit because I loved fresh food. Ryan and I planted a small garden in Michigan, and when we moved, tending the garden became part of his responsibilities. This shift occurred after we had our youngest, Annabelle, because a newborn obviously kept me busy, and then continued because Ryan grew to enjoy gardening. The simple tasks became a way for him to relax and unwind—plowing the dirt, planting the seedlings, transferring the fragile plants to freshly mixed dirt and compost, watering the plants, weeding, and eventually, the fun part, picking the hard-earned produce.

Ryan has unexpectedly discovered that not only does he have a knack for organic gardening, but also a successful garden takes a lot of work! Especially when it comes to controlling the weeds without harsh chemicals—which we avoid. During long summer days, we recruit the kids to help. Some enjoy it; a few others complain and mumble about how unfair life is and sing "It's a Hard Knock Life" as they pull weeds. Anything worth having requires work—including fresh, organic veggies. The garden becomes a team-building exercise, as each family member pulls the weeds in their designated spot, giving the plants the opportunity to grow and produce; however, if a helper becomes lazy and decides to simply make it appear as if the weeding was accomplished, failing to pull the invaders out by the root, that individual will have a mess to face in a day or two when those roots regrow and multiply.

Marriage is a lot like a garden.

There's a popular theory that states how people often choose a spouse based on how an individual is able to shine a light on the weeds in their life. The person we chose to spend the rest of our life with supposedly mirrors our insecurities, doubts, and unresolved childhood issues, and as those issues rise to the surface, we can address them in a healthy way, yank them out by the roots by getting to the bottom of the issue, or dismiss the issues, in turn preventing growth. These resentment weeds will continue to grow with heated arguments, unforgiveness, or lack of communication—and they will suck the life out of marriage quickly if left unaddressed.

I initially had a difficult time letting Ryan into my heart. I was a good wife. A loving wife. I supported him and did the things good wives do, such as preparing dinner, cleaning the house, and making sure his dirty clothes were run through the washing machine. But I was emotionally closed off for a long time and didn't grant him full access to my heart. Because of Jason's death, I have abandonment issues. And because of my experiences with both Lucas and Jason, I have control issues, and these issues often result in a lack of trust, which leads me to shut my heart to those I love.

The first step has been acknowledging that there is a weed in my life, because without acknowledgment there cannot be change. The conversations have been difficult—who wants to say to their spouse, *You know honey, I think I really have a problem with anger? Or addiction? Or boundaries? Or control?* Some of the most difficult words to say are admitting our own weaknesses! But here's the thing—our spouse is probably already aware of our shortcomings and is patiently waiting for us to invite them into our struggles so they can join the fight for a better marriage.

Through honest communication, meaningful time together, getting outside help when needed, and extending forgiveness, we have the ability to control many of the weeds in the marital garden and, in the process, cultivate the growth of a truly meaningful relationship.

Chicken Fajitas

Our garden stocks our freezer and pantry full of pizza and spaghetti sauces, pickled jalapenos, squash relish (which is delicious!), and fresh peppers. We like to throw our peppers into casseroles, put them on pizzas, and include them in one of our favorite meals—chicken fajitas.

- 4–8 chicken breasts
- 1 bottle of Italian dressing
- 1 packet of taco seasoning
- Salt and pepper to taste

- A few tbsp of olive oil
- An assortment of peppers, sliced
- 2 yellow onions, sliced thin
- Tortillas (corn or flour)
- Toppings (salsa, sour cream, cheese, lettuce, and/or tomatoes)

Prick the chicken with a fork and then marinate it in the Italian dressing for a few hours. Place it on the grill or in a cast-iron skillet (with a few tablespoons of olive oil), season with salt and pepper, and cook until the middle is no longer pink. Let it cool for about 10 minutes, and then slice it into strips. In the meantime, toss the peppers and onions in a skillet along with some olive oil. Season with salt, pepper, and taco seasoning. Cook until soft—but not too soft! You don't want them to end up mushy. Throw the chicken in the skillet for a minute, coating it with all the seasonings. Add some of the chicken, onion, and pepper mixture to a tortilla and pile on your favorite toppings. Enjoy!

Dock the Boat: The Comingling of Grief and Joy

Grief shows up in the strangest ways. I can be completely at peace, and a thought will emerge out of nowhere. Suddenly, I'm back in hospice with Jason or scared and pregnant with Lucas. Grief manifests in unlikely ways, such as eating a whole bag of Cheetos in an afternoon or maybe instigating a blowout argument with Ryan over whose turn it is to bathe the kids. It might be popping a few Advil because my head won't stop pounding or crawling into bed at 8:00 p.m. and not getting out again until noon the next day. Sometimes it's serving cereal for dinner seven nights in a row or having that extra cocktail, even though I know I shouldn't. Maybe it's organizing the entire house—all the closets and cupboards—and making ten trips to Goodwill to avoid thinking. Or perhaps it's choosing a song that I know will ignite the waterworks and soaking in the pain, rather than tapping my feet to the joyful beat.

Grief is a strange and unpredictable force that must be recognized for what it is and given its proper place in life—like a river that rages at times and calmly flows at other times. It's a part of us, the river, part of the experience necessary for life—as is the boat we cling to as the water bends us to its will, the boat that provides safety—or is it, perhaps, captivity?

We can always choose to row toward the shore, exit the boat, and sink our weary feet into the mossy ground. Maybe we build a home and create a life with those we love—a life beside the waters, with our boat docked by the shore as we remember our time on the river, expressing gratefulness that the boat no longer serves as a life preserver or a prison. We might learn to dance again, slowly allowing our feet to reclaim their joy as we dance beside the cool, calm stream—a dance of remembrance and thankfulness as the river continues to ebb and flow, the river which holds our experiences of joy and pain. These are options we have—options that affect our relationships with those we love: our spouses, children, and friends.

There is a time for everything.

A time to weep and a time to laugh.

A time to mourn and a time to dance.

A time to leave the boat. A time to rise above the pain of the past. A time to choose joy.

It's always a choice. A choice to create a life with those we love, a choice to grow food and prepare meals and gather around the table. A choice to see the good in one another and a choice to dance—or we can choose to climb back into the boat and leave, trying our luck on the river once again, trying our luck on greener grass around the river bend. And, at first, as we row out, the river may feel like a peaceful reprieve, a break, but as night falls and the wind turns gusty, the river's peace is traded for tumultuous waters that no longer feel like a break but instead remind us of our pain or perhaps introduce new layers of grief, and we yearn to return to the comfort of those we know. The safety and security provided by our home.

Blended life can be incredibly difficult and is filled with layers of grief and joy—the past overflowing with lost dreams, now-buried dreams of a traditional family with two loving parents, each parent invested in the well-being of their offspring. Joy abounds when love is found, but that joy is quickly soured when stepchildren yell hateful threats or refuse to listen to the "new" mom. Time is our ally in this thing called life—be it blended or traditional or single life. Each day, each moment, adds up to chunks of time that will make a difference. These moments become years, and these years create memories, and memories create roots, and these roots will firmly ground a family when given time. Firmly ground your family on high ground beside the river, with roots that will enable your family to ultimately flourish and bloom.

Enjoy those times away on the boat—those early days wrestling with the meaning of the pain, cursing life and those who you may blame for causing you deep scars. Those are valuable times, as we sway to the beat of the river's bend in moments of self-care and reflection—but then choose (yes, choose) to rise up out of the boat and face another day with your loved ones on the shore. The journey is well worth it as you welcome God's love and abundance into your life.

5

EMBRACING THE UNIQUE BEAUTY OF YOUR FAMILY

How to *Address* Special Circumstances and *Do* What Works

In 2004, I went to what I assumed would be a routine twenty-week ultrasound appointment for my second child. I went alone because my husband Jason stayed home to care for our two-year-old son Caleb.

I propped myself up on the cold table that dreary May morning, contact paper crinkling beneath me as rain pelted against the brick building. The nurse slowly maneuvered the wand across my belly, unable to meet my eyes.

"I'll be right back," she whispered. "I have to find the doctor."

Those six words reverberated in my thoughts for years and began a continuous cycle of fear related to pregnancy and ultrasound appointments.

The doctor arrived and immediately dove into the unexpected news: "Your baby suffered a stroke, which has caused severe fluid buildup in the brain. These babies rarely make it. You should terminate and try again. You are young and healthy, and won't have any problems getting pregnant."

Shell-shocked and numb after hearing the news, I gathered my belongings and drove home, where I found my husband Jason praying for my safety. He and I refused to accept death for our child, keeping faith that God would intervene and heal our unborn baby.

August 12, 2004. I held my breath as I waited on the sterile table, my belly ripped open from one side to the other to accommodate my baby's large head, thoughts racing, back and forth and back and forth like the tennis balls my husband often hit on the weekends during practice. Suddenly, there was a hardy cry as the baby was gently lifted from the gaping hole. God had heard my desperate pleas, and my Lucas was alive. My August 19, 2004, journal entry reads:

> Baby Lucas is one week old today. He is beautiful. My heartbeat and God's greatest teacher to me.

The birth of Lucas brought forth a new era of aimlessly roaming, lost, in unfamiliar territory—a terrain of special-needs parenting where milestones weren't normal and exceptions to the norm were the rule of the land—a place where I relied heavily on God's peace and wisdom as Jason and I made important, life-altering decisions for our family.

There were numerous fears of the unknown, and I asked countless questions at every appointment we attended:

What is the life expectancy of a child like this?
How often do kids like Lucas have shunt malfunctions?
Will his head size ever decrease?
Will he walk?

Have you ever witnessed a case where a hydrocephalic person's body miraculously healed itself?

During this period of uncertainty, I often sought to control what I could. I was convinced that if I had enough knowledge or spoke enough words of faith to move the mountain of fluid in my son's head, I would then receive the outcome I desired—complete healing, a "normal" baby, a typical child through and through. My philosophy was to speak the right magical words, have the right amount of faith (which really isn't all that much according to Christ . . . only a mustard seed!), find the right specialists, and try this or that natural potion. It all proved to be exhausting, especially with a child who never slept!

My fears grew and began to fester, and instead of allowing God's Word to hold my thoughts captive and provide peace, I allowed fear to strangle and suffocate my heart. All four pregnancies after Lucas were saturated with fear from the moment the child was conceived until the moment I gave birth (or miscarried, in one instance). I never enjoyed a pregnancy again after Lucas. Every day became a battle as I replayed worst-case scenarios in my mind.

My definition of fear is this: *Allowing future worries to ruin today.*

How many days, weeks, and months were ruined because of fear? Goodness, multiply my four pregnancies times nine months and that's a bunch of days!

It's been a long, slow process of learning to release the perception that I have control in life—yes, *perception*. At forty-three years old, I live in the present more effectively than I ever have before, and hopefully I can see more improvement at eighty-six!

We are again smack-dab in the middle of a season of change, with numerous life-altering decisions on the horizon. Caleb and Tate are entering their senior year of high school and will graduate by the time this book hits the press. Two rockets we are launching out into the world! We have decisions to make about Lucas's future and where we will find resources for him as he ages. Ryan is in the middle of a career change, and I probably won't return to my former profession of teaching because between nonprofit work and writing and eight children, something has to be cut loose. I have very little control and feel entirely at the Lord's mercy about the timing of many of these decisions.

What I have found helpful is to focus on the present, this day, and what I'm thankful for in these moments. For example, as I type these words, we are twelve weeks into quarantine with eight children due to the worldwide COVID-19 pandemic. If there are parts of this book that seem absolutely ridiculous, we'll blame it on this reality. Twelve weeks of isolation, exhaustion, and bored children. Lucas's entire life was uprooted, and he doesn't understand why. Twelve weeks of working and writing in complete chaos, and often the worry consumes me, and I start to wonder:

What if we're never released from quarantine?
What if these children live here forever?
What if Ryan can't start his new career, and we go broke?
What if Ryan's properties never sell because Realtors can't show houses?
What if we have to live in a box and Lucas screams "All done!" every day and night?

And on and on and on.

But then I pause.

Today.

Live in the present.

Not tomorrow. Today. This present moment is all I need to be concerned with. And I readjust and center my thoughts as I meditate on what I'm thankful for right now.

We have a beautiful home. We are healthy. Lucas has settled into his new routine. The sun has been shining! I get to write books for a living—my dream job!

And this spirit of thankfulness grounds me and serves as a reminder that when my focus is turned to how God has already taken care of my needs, I'm then able to trust that he will supply my needs in the future—manna for the moment.

Fear has a way of making decisions it has no business making. Release this harmful emotion and lean into God's grace—moment by moment—relying on his peace and strength to sustain. Truly learn to embody the wisdom of Matthew 6:34: "Do not worry about tomorrow for tomorrow will worry about itself. Each day has enough trouble of its own." Period.

Lucas Aaron: Special Needs Is Challenging, but There Is Joy in Obedience

Raising a child with special needs is an exhausting endeavor. There are currently 65 million caregivers in the United States, and 16.8 million of these individuals are caring for a child with special needs—that's 15 percent of the population. Twenty-three percent of caregivers report that caring for a loved one has led to poor health, and the level of stress related to caregiving can take up to ten years off a person's life. Yikes.

A few years ago, an acquaintance's young daughter unexpectedly passed away. This little girl was never supposed to live for more than a few hours; however, kids often have a way of proving the experts wrong. After she died, I asked her momma if the new ease of life haunted her, because when you live entrenched in special needs, there are rarely moments of peace. Life as a caregiver is often compared to being in a combat zone, constantly anticipating your child's next basic needs—hunger, pain, angst, smells, what, where, when, why—all the time. Many special-needs children remain completely dependent on others their entire lives, which means there is no end in sight, and that can be a daunting truth for an aging caregiver.

This momma paused and considered my question and then quietly agreed. The peace and quiet did have an ominous feel, but she also missed the unadulterated joy she experienced while caring for her daughter. She missed the meaning of the caregiving experience so much that she is now in the process of adopting a little girl with special needs.

> The King will reply, "Truly I tell you, whatever you did for one of the least of these brothers and sisters of mine, you did for me." (Matt. 25:40)

These children, the Lucases of the world, are the least of the least of the least of these. They often have the mental and emotional capacity of an infant. They are unable to care for themselves without continual assistance, and without the loving intervention of caregivers, these children would not survive. Some of the ways these individuals require care include bathing; feeding (either by utensil or tube feeding), which is often accomplished in a special chair; diapering; restraining a teenager who has become aggressive due to puberty; visiting the local emergency room at midnight to play a guessing game to determine the cause of angst in a nonverbal child; declining an invitation to an event because there is no one who is willing to watch your child; attempting to distract a child who is frustrated and banging his head as a self-soothing technique; sleeping with a baby monitor for eighteen years or more; getting up multiple times throughout the night to administer medications, tubes, or breathing equipment, or to make sure your child is still alive; spending most of your free time in a doctor's or therapist's office; not being alone with your spouse for years because there is no one to care for your child in your absence; or suffering from extreme pain and popping Advil like candy because your child has grown too large for you to comfortably handle and the strain has taken a toll on your aging body. These are just a few examples.

Most people can't understand how difficult Lucas is at sixteen years old. The restlessness, high-pitched screams when he can't communicate his needs, side effects of puberty, incontinence, and inability to verbalize what he wants (or even understand what he desires) make it a huge undertaking to raise this unique child, but I do it. I go through the motions and thank God for giving me a child who has taught me valuable lessons throughout his fragile life. But it's still hard.

In December 2019, Lucas was admitted to the ICU for what would become a month-long hospital stay as he battled a shunt infection, and I was given a glimpse at a different life—much like Nicholas Cage experienced in the beloved movie *Family Man*. A thirty-day glimpse of a different life. Not a life in the ICU, with beeping machines and lifesaving equipment, but a life at home, away from the beeping machines, a life I returned to after Ryan relieved me at the hospital, a life with Lucas's siblings. A life where I awoke to the rising of the sun and not to my sixteen-year-old screaming over the baby monitor. A life where I had the freedom to run to the store for milk and not worry about who would stay with Lucas. A life where I didn't have to constantly decipher what my nonverbal child wanted, and a life void of diapers and wheelchairs and walls smeared with food wherever he ate his last meal.

An easier life. A life of peace or more peace than I was used to. A life of occasional silence. A life without Lucas.

Struggle has a way of forcing beauty to the surface. I think about the pink desert cactus planted in a dry, parched land—sinking its roots deeply into the brittle soil, willing its way to the surface. Beyond the menacing thorns, the bright-pink petals unfold in majestic glory as the soul reaches for the sun. Obedience to what God has asked of us also produces beauty—forged through a cracked and desolate path. On the surface, these hard and holy treasures may seem but dull nuggets containing what really matters—love, joy, patience, kindness, and service to others. They are unearthed as glittering jewels through trauma and agonizing moans and breaths that can't be released and heartache that brought me to my knees as I begged God to intervene and heal my son during those stressful days apart.

I wrestled with the Almighty for days as Lucas lay in the ICU, revisiting familiar ground from sixteen years prior as his fragile body grew in my belly. There was weeping, moaning, begging, and my thoughts were frightening, laced with guilt: *There's peace. It's quiet. My heart isn't racing. I slept all night. . . .*

Beside the cords and tubes and beeping machines, sweat dripping from my brow, I pleaded with God:

> *Father, grant me the strength to endure the hard, screaming, physically, emotionally, and spiritually draining cup you have asked of me to drink. Please spare my son. I choose him. I choose the difficult path you have called me to walk. I choose life. Give me grace and strength to walk the road. Crucify every desire for prideful control. May I serve the least of these in your kingdom, and may I serve them joyfully. "Yet not my will, but yours be done" (Luke 22:42).*

Lucas is my road, my journey. I choose the narrow, parched path, where only pink petals bloom. The path is lined with thorns and littered with dull and dirty nuggets—nuggets that mask a priceless treasure beneath the dirt and the grime and the walls smeared with food. I choose hard and holy, and it chooses me. I choose Lucas again and again and again, as did my friend who is now adopting. There is beauty in obedience and growth in continuously laying down your life to serve someone who cannot care for himself. I am engaged in holy work, and it is a privilege to witness tiny glimpses of heaven, beautiful pink petals, through the beauty of raising my boy.

Lucas's Favorite Zucchini Boats

Due to texture issues, I am always, always, always trying to find sneaky ways to get Lucas to eat healthy foods. He does love anything that resembles lasagna; thus zucchini boats were created!

- 1 pound of ground hamburger
- 1 pound of ground sausage
- 3–5 whole zucchini
- 2 6-ounce cans of tomato paste
- 1 onion, diced
- 4–6 cloves of garlic, minced
- 1 tsp oregano
- 2 cups mozzarella, shredded (or nutritional yeast for a dairy-free option)
- 2 14-ounce cans of tomatoes
- Salt and pepper to taste
- 2–3 tbsp olive oil

Preheat the oven to 400 degrees. Cut off the ends of the zucchini and then cut them in half. Spoon the seeds out of the middle. Brush a little olive oil on the insides, and season them with salt and pepper. Place them on a cookie sheet and cook them for 15–20 minutes. Remove and allow them to cool. Place a skillet over medium-high heat and add extra-virgin olive oil. Once hot, add the onion and garlic. Cook until the onion starts to soften. Add the hamburger and sausage, and cook until browned. Drain off any excess fat, return the mixture to skillet, then add the rest of the ingredients. Mix everything, and let it simmer on low heat for 30 minutes. Spoon the filling into the zucchini. Top with cheese or dairy-free nutritional yeast. Place, uncovered, into a 350-degree oven and cook for 20-25 minutes until the cheese is golden brown.

Church at the Park: Setting Aside Expectations and Doing What Works for Your Family

I'm a woman of faith. My faith has changed, morphed, transformed, wavered, staggered, grown, and matured through the years, and often all at the same time! But what remains is this truth—I have a deep, abiding faith in a being higher than myself, and I believe this being (I like the words *The Almighty*) has led and directed me to this moment in time, to my beautiful family, and I trust that he (or she) will continue to transform and change and morph and grow a good work in me until the day I die.

Ryan and I entered our marriage with similar religious backgrounds—meaning that he and I, for the most part, saw eye to eye when it came to our faith practices. The premises of our beliefs were closely aligned, and we approached our faith with an open mind, which made the transition as a new family easier.

After our honeymoon, we immediately began attending my church, Mars Hill Bible Church in Grand Rapids, Michigan. The kids enjoyed it because bagels were served before the service. (They are easily swayed by free food, as are we, with our large crew.) The teaching was inspiring, the people were kind, and they offered an entire ministry devoted to children with special needs, which was a big perk with Lucas. We stayed there for a year, and then the church experienced a restructuring period, and we made the decision to find a new place of worship—something that was uniquely ours instead of being tied to my past.

Many of my associations and memories at Mars Hill were painful, and I often experienced flashbacks as I sat in the pew on Sunday morning. Jason had rapidly deteriorated during our period at this church—slowly losing his battle with cancer as vision loss and an inability to walk set in toward the end of his life. Also, people knew me, knew that I had lost my husband, and knew my children had recently lost their father, which led to many confused questions (and I'm sure many unspoken thoughts) concerning whether or not I had maybe lost my mind as I walked in the doors with a new guy and three new children shortly after Jason's death. We needed a fresh start. We found a wonderful option fifteen minutes from our house that also offered a special-needs ministry and an energetic children's program. We enjoyed our time there until we moved to rural Tennessee, and then church became an actual issue.

Rural America doesn't offer many options for special-needs families, and we tried almost every church within a thirty-mile radius: Baptist (every First Baptist we could find), nondenominational, Presbyterian, and a beautiful old Methodist church where the pastor invited Christ's presence into the sanctuary by ringing bells. Attending a new church every week for months with our crew became quite the task, and the kids would moan and groan, "Why do we have to try another church? Can't we just skip it?"

We began to wonder the same thing: "Can't we just skip it?" And on a few hot summer days, we would. We'd toss our church clothes back into the closet, and instead of scoping out another sanctuary, we'd head to the park for a picnic. A park that was transformed into a water park on really hot days. A park where we ate homemade chicken salad heaped high on croissants. A park where, if I didn't get around to making chicken salad, we instead settled for cheap pizzas. A park where the kids laughed and ran and played nonstop—and had to be reminded to drink from the water fountain, lest they become dehydrated. A park where football and kickball were in full force as Dad reverted back to the hotshot teenager he once was—showing his teenage boys exactly who's in charge. A park where our baby, Annabelle, played so hard she was dripping with sweat and exhausted by the time we loaded into our van to begin the trek back home. A park where Lucas walked and played and shimmied down slide after slide, swaying his head and smiling in delight as he hollered, "Go whee!" A park where we watched in holy awe, taking in the miracle—little Lucas, now big Lucas, walking, talking, and having fun with us, his family, and thanking Jesus for his faithfulness. Thanking Jesus for our church at the park. I believe in the value of community and worshipping with believers, but I also believe there are seasons in life where that isn't optimal.

I look back on my season when Jason was fighting brain cancer, slowly dying, unable to orient himself at church and me guiding him and Lucas as I pushed Joshua in a stroller and Caleb tagged along behind, holding Mabel's hand. I arose, each Sunday morning, because of the expectation that I *had* to be in church, and I should have instead allowed myself grace. Grace to say no. Grace to say, "This doesn't work for our family right now." I should have instead allowed the shepherd to lead me to green pastures where I could have promptly taken a nap: "He makes me lie down in green pastures" (Ps. 23:2). That would have been a more appropriate version of church in those days, and it would have restored my soul. Instead, I had to show up, in church, on the verge of tears if anyone talked to me. I had to show up for false expectations that I was holding it all together, still in control, when I obviously wasn't. It was my pride that drove me there, drove me to show off how I was "managing just fine," and pride that wouldn't allow myself grace.

I still pray for a real church someday—a body of believers to gather with. I long for it, but in the meantime, we're content with Christ's invitation to worship at the park if that's what obedience to Jesus looks like for a period of time.

Chicken Salad Sandwiches

I love making this chicken salad on Saturday and letting the flavors come together overnight for our picnic days at the park. It's a really simple dish with loads of flavor. Add grapes too, if that's your thing.

- 1 whole chicken, rinsed and patted dry
- Salt and pepper to taste
- 1 large lemon
- 1 large onion, chopped
- A jar of pickle relish (sweet or dill depending on preference)
- 1–2 tsp paprika
- 1 tsp cayenne pepper (omit if you don't like it spicy)
- 1 tsp dry mustard
- Slivered almonds
- Salt and pepper to taste
- Mayo to taste

Place the chicken in a roasting pan. Rub lemon juice all over the chicken, and season it with salt and pepper. Bake covered overnight at 200 degrees. In the morning, remove the chicken and allow it to cool. Then cut it into bite-sized pieces (saving the bones for bone broth), and place it in a large bowl. Add the remaining ingredients and cool the mixture in the fridge for a few hours. This is another great example of mixing a few simple ingredients together and then letting the flavors meld together over time in the fridge to create a delicious sandwich spread.

Siblings and Special Needs: "Mom! Don't Bring Lucas!"

On a particularly warm summer day in June, Ryan and I announced to our crew: "Kids! You've been so helpful lately and completed your chores without complaining, so we're going to have a family fun day at a water park!"

Our children responded with glee and excitement and *Yays!* and then asked, "Who's going to watch Lucas?"

"We're going to bring him," we replied. "He'll enjoy getting out of the house."

"Mom! *No!*" bellowed the sounds of despair. "We'll have to leave early if he comes!"

This is a constant dilemma in our life.

We brought him. He did make it very difficult and tiring. We had to leave early because Ryan and I were beyond beat after a few hours of fun. We arrived around 11:00 a.m. for an event with free food—a major bonus for our crew. We piled ten plates full of grub, and Ryan retreated to the shade to feed Lucas, away from people, to eliminate the prospect of overstimulation and to ensure that he wouldn't grab food from others. I found a table near the hot dogs because I knew my crew was going to take advantage of the free factor. Mya took charge of Annabelle as she skited about, and the rest were free to roam independently. A word here—at this point, Lucas was (and still is) no longer content to sit. *Ever*. He has declared a mutiny on his stroller and wants nothing to do with it, but he continues to require constant supervision for his and others' safety. Ryan and I traded twenty-minute intervals introducing him to a plethora of activities—five slides, water features, an accessible swing, acres of land to explore, and unlimited hotdogs, which was the highlight of his day.

About three hours later, we looked at each other and we knew. We knew we were done. Physically, mentally, and emotionally. And we also knew our kids wouldn't be happy about our decision.

"Let's give them the thirty-minute warning," my wise husband suggested.

We did.

The moans of disappointment began: "Lucas always makes us leave early!" "Why can't we find a babysitter for him?" "Why can't you and dad drive separately?" (Perhaps we should have, but the park was forty-five minutes from our house.) "*Why do we have to bring him?!*"

They wailed.

And we responded, just as frustrated as they were and exhausted, questioning the validity of the excuse we offered: "Because he's part of our family, and sometimes we need to include him."

We currently do not have a solution for this problem. It is what it is. We feel the need to include Lucas—even at the expense of his siblings' happiness—but we understand their frustration.

I was recently asked by a well-meaning person, "Do you feel like your other kids are slighted because Lucas requires so much time and energy?"

It was a valid question, but it irked me a little bit because we really don't have a choice in the matter. As I thought about it, I understood why the question was asked, and the answer is complex but overall, no, I don't.

I don't believe my children are slighted because of Lucas, and instead, I believe their lives and their contribution to humanity will only increase because he is their brother. Their souls possess layers of kindness and love and patience and grace, and their stories will also hold these values as they grow and walk through the world, and this is a good story to have—especially in our current narcissistic culture. It's a story any parent would want for their child. Not a self-centered narrative that plagues many children these days—no, a story of compassion and mercy. A story of endurance. A story of being the hands and feet of Jesus to the least of these. My children, Lucas's brothers and sisters, have all the things in life that are important: faith, a roof over their heads, food, siblings to play with—and lots and lots of love. That's their story, and Lucas only increases the good; he doesn't detract from it.

I don't have all the answers for this kind of dilemma—only suggestions. We do recognize the need for our seven typical children to have time with Mom and Dad without special-needs concerns. Lucas requires an immense amount of energy, and it's not fair if we're always exhausted because our limited energy is spent on his care. Here are a few ways we've tried to remedy our situation.

Vacation Minus One

Lucas doesn't go on vacation with us. Jason and I once planned a fun family vacation with Caleb and Lucas in Frankenmuth, Michigan, the Christmas capital of the world. We checked into our hotel room and then had an enjoyable evening at a local restaurant and enjoyed the sights at the world's largest Christmas store. Then it was bedtime. We laid Caleb down, and we tried to lay two-year-old Lucas in his playpen, but he proceeded to scream until 1:00 a.m. because it wasn't his normal environment. So we packed up and drove two hours back home because we were concerned he would annoy every occupant in the hotel that night. We attempted a few more vacations with him throughout the years, and every single one ended in a disaster because Lucas doesn't appreciate new environments or experiences. When he was around eight or nine years old, I finally allowed myself permission to say "We don't have to take him on vacations anymore."

Family Days

We sometimes have a similar perspective with family fun day. We do bring Lucas occasionally, but we've recognized that this often has more to do with saving face ("See, we're including Lucas!") than it has to do with actually benefitting our son. As I stated before, Lucas doesn't like new environments. I understand the value in introducing new ideas or people or environments into his life for his growth, but he doesn't personally require it. It took years and many, many failed attempts at family fun to allow ourselves permission to realize that he doesn't need to be included in everything.

Reaching Out for Help When It's Needed

We do ask that Lucas's siblings occasionally help with his care. Over summer break, it's mandatory for each sibling to engage in a fifteen-minute peer buddy time with him each day. We also "hire" them to help feed him or take him for walks. This not only strengthens their bond with their brother (and his bond with them) but makes us a stronger family unit, as we stress the importance of helping one another.

Manna for the Moment: Prioritizing Self-Care to Combat Caregiver Stress and PTSD

As I write this, Lucas has been back in school for a week—a week post–summer break. Summer break is always an immensely difficult time for him and has become especially challenging as he ages. When he was little, more manageable, not prone to outbursts, and not yet a full-grown man-child in diapers, we could easily employ care for him. Young college girls didn't have a problem watching an adorable four-year-old in diapers, but now that he's older and stronger and pimply, those college girls are no longer interested, and summer camps and daycares have restrictions on sixteen-year-olds in diapers. This lonely reality is an overwhelming burden on caregivers because children like Lucas thrive in structure, and when the structure is abruptly removed—via the end of the school year—they are lost, confused, and bored.

Lucas isn't capable of accomplishing life skills independently and needs assistance with almost every aspect of life: bathing, feeding, diapering, and moving from one space to another. He also requires constant supervision or a safe, restrictive place where he can sit with his iPad, watch videos, and play with his toys. We've been able to create this space for him, but it isn't a permanent solution as he matures and grows. He has testosterone flowing through his body, just like any other sixteen-year-old boy, and he doesn't know how to cope with his feelings of aggression and angst. He can't call his friends and suggest a game of football or release his restlessness through physical activity. His frustration often manifests through excessive screaming, silent head banging, or a lack of decisiveness when he cannot adequately convey his desires or he doesn't even completely understand what he wants. This lack of communication is a huge hindrance to his happiness and our ability as his caregivers to satisfy him.

Experts claim that special-needs caregivers experience post-traumatic stress disorder (PTSD)—a disorder usually associated with veterans who have experienced traumatic events during wartime. I particularly notice this PTSD tendency when I don't have Lucas on my radar for a period of time. Like now. With his return to school Monday through Friday, I've finally returned to work: writing, preparing for the classes I teach, flitting from here to there, ordering groceries on Instacart, watering flowers on the patio, going about my day, and then I stop . . .

About every thirty minutes or so, I ignore the sounds around me—the whir of the washing machine, the chattering of my four-year-old, and the constant buzz of lawnmowers outside. I ignore the background noise and selectively lean my ear toward the basement. I listen intently for Lucas and wait for one of his normal, loud requests: "All done!" or (lately) "Wiggles!" which means "I don't like what I'm doing or watching, so please offer five hundred additional options, and then I'll agree to one of them by telling you, 'Bye-bye!'" Or I wander aimlessly to my bedroom, where I check the 24/7 surveillance monitor, but there are no high-pitched screams and the image is empty. Or every few hours I find myself in Lucas's room, lost, having forgotten what I came down for. My body can't release the summer routine, and I inhale deeply—quickly checking for any indication that there may be a diaper to change—but there isn't. I forgot again. Lucas is at school. There are only the remains of his favorites: his iPad (in need of charging before he arrives home) and numerous sippy cups scattered about that need cleaning (the only cups he will drink from).

And like clockwork, morning, noon, and night, I ask myself, *What am I going to feed Lucas today, and do we have those ingredients?* Due to texture issues, I often prepare his meals separately, and because of my desire for him to eat healthy food, I will go the extra mile to hide the zucchini and green beans.

This is the process of PTSD for me, for caregivers—always being on, always having our senses at high alert, always being at the beck and call of another. It is a refining process like no other, a constant laying down of our life and our desires for someone who is unable to care for him- or herself. It is a holy calling, but it is an exhaustive undertaking. It takes patience and self-care and sometimes righteous anger and unrelenting faith—faith in the meaning beyond ourselves. Because that's why we do it, right? That's why we rise to the calling and fulfill the mundane and monotonous tasks day in and day out, isn't it?

And somehow, gloriously (miraculously, really), as the sun appears, or maybe it doesn't some days, we are greeted yet again with the gift of time, which will bring fresh grace and new mercies served alongside lots of lukewarm coffee as we hurriedly offer a familiar prayer—*Give us this day our daily bread*—like fresh manna from heaven, manna for the moment, and that is enough. It has to be enough.

TAKEAWAYS

(ESPECIALLY FOR CAREGIVERS)

- Invite Jesus into the daily struggle—preferably in the morning. Upon waking, the first words I whisper are *Jesus, give me grace and strength.* It sets the tone for my heart and day.
- Ask for help. Find a tribe and be truthful about how difficult and lonely the journey can be. I believe that people want to help, but if we hide behind the fake pretense that all is well, people won't know! And if they don't know, they can't help.
- *Take time for self-care!* Carve it out one way or another—it is truly life changing. This can be a walk in the morning, a chat with a good friend, yoga at the gym (all my favorites), or whatever makes you smile. Get over the mom guilt and understand this fact: You are doing no one any favors by not making yourself a daily priority. You will be a better person and able to sustain the intense demands of caring for a child in a more compassionate way.
- Find community. Depression breeds in isolation. We need other people to help carry our burdens.
- Finally, if you struggle with suicidal thoughts, thoughts of harming yourself or your child, or are self-medicating through drugs or alcohol, please seek professional help immediately. Remember: You are never in this alone.

6

EVERYTHING TAKES TIME

Keeping the *Faith* When Life Gives You *Lemons*

It hurts like hell
It stings
It falls so painfully short of what we feel this
life should be
It aches like betrayal on a massive scale
A worldwide scale
And we, in our frail humanity, are the victims
left in the wake
A big joke played on all
By a bunch of pranksters residing in the heavenlies
And forgotten yesterdays
And the vacant present
And there are still no answers
The Creator is silent
The baby remains absent

I wrote these words after my beloved unborn baby was finally released from my body after miscarrying for three months.

Ryan and I were 100 percent certain we did not want any more children. And then my sister got pregnant. And then my sister-in-law had an "oops." And then our babies, Josh and Jada, grew up, and they weren't so difficult anymore. Our family solidified with the move to rural Tennessee, and we matured and understood each other better. Therapy helped us work through hard relational issues, and Ryan and I were mastering the art of communicating with each other. And then I looked at him one day and jokingly said, "We should have a baby!"

I was joking because he had a vasectomy prior to our wedding; we were *that* certain a future pregnancy was not in the plan. And as I released those words, "We should have a baby!" my husband scooped my face into his tender hands and replied, "I always wanted to have a baby with you."

And now I was alone, scared, and full of despair as I mourned a baby that had almost become a reality and now, again, was simply a dream. I could not understand why God wouldn't bless me with a healthy baby—especially after all I had been through, especially after obeying what he had called me to do in blending my family and raising seven beautiful but tiring children. I deserved this baby!

The whole idea of pregnancy seemed like a relatively simple plan, right? Have sex and ta-da! Two pink lines appear! At least that's how it happened in my twenties, but it was not so simple as a thirty-six-year-old. I was in a new state with a new doctor who spoke really fast and didn't have time for questions. This doctor was also ninety miles from where I lived, which made appointments difficult to schedule and babysitters hard to find.

After a few stressful months of trying to conceive, I was ecstatic to see those promising pink lines indicating success. Ryan and the kids were equally as excited, and we immediately announced our joy to everyone with a big Facebook announcement. The pregnancy was normal—at least what had historically been normal for me. I was nauseous, tired, and bemoaning the fact that I had breath in my lungs at six and seven weeks, and then at eight weeks, on a girl's trip in St. Louis with Mabel and Mya, I suddenly felt fine.

I had never felt any semblance of normalcy with my other four pregnancies until the fourteen-week marker, and I was scared. I ordered club sandwiches everywhere—trying to induce nausea with meat that had always caused an immediate gag reflex in the past, but the sandwiches didn't have the same effect this time. They were tasty. I tearfully called Ryan as I watched my daughters enjoy the unlimited breakfast buffet at our hotel: "I'm pretty sure we lost the baby," I whispered as people hustled by, unaware of the private hell I was experiencing.

"Honey, it'll be fine," he reassured me. "You're having a different experience this time. Different sperm," he nervously laughed.

But I knew better.

I arrived home and immediately scheduled a doctor's appointment. The doctor couldn't find a heartbeat, but I was told not to worry because it was still early. A week later, there was blood. We rushed to the ER, where we discovered that the baby was gone.

The following night, we gathered the kids for a family meeting to share the news, but I couldn't speak. I stared at the floor as tears leaked out of the corners of my eyes. Tate glanced at me, trying to be brave as tears threatened to spill down his face, and said, "The baby died, right?"

The doctor insisted that my body would eventually let go of our unborn child but, as I'd learned with Lucas, my body doesn't let go easily. It instead hangs on for dear life. I would bleed for three months.

And here I was now, on the cold bathroom floor, weeping over what I thought was the end and being somewhat at peace with the process because we could finally have the conversation about trying again. I sat upright, composed myself, and left to find a plastic Walmart bag. I re-entered the bathroom and lovingly gathered the bloody toilet paper that I had thrown into the wastebasket, gently placing each piece into the plastic sack. I wiped tears from my bloodshot eyes and silently walked out the front door. I was headed to the cemetery on our property—yes, our private cemetery. On the way, I grabbed a shovel from the garage before trekking up the steep hill, behind the trees, and into the gated plot. I knelt and buried those bloodied tissues, tears gushing as blood and snot intermingled and I placed a large rock on top of the dirt—a rock which would later be painted by the kids in remembrance of their unborn sibling.

I stayed for a moment and knelt beside the makeshift grave, silent. I stayed to honor the pain with my presence. I stayed to feel the agony, and I allowed it to strengthen me as I resolved to keep moving forward.

In hindsight, God used our next nine months of waiting to become pregnant again as an opportunity to birth something beautiful in my marriage, as Ryan and I gained a deeper intimacy which preceded the conception of our eighth child—our beautiful daughter, Annabelle Ryan. God is good. All the time. And sometimes pain forces obedience to his plan.

Grief is a vague concept with no end, but the burden does lighten with time. I will always mourn the child I never knew, but now when I look at my beautiful daughter Annabelle, that awful experience doesn't sting because without that loss, I would lose her, and I can't imagine a life without her. I feel the same about Jason's death. I will always mourn his loss, but without his death, I would lose five people who I can't imagine my life without: Ryan, Tate, Mya, Jada, and Annabelle.

C. S. Lewis offers a profound statement in *A Grief Observed*, written after his beloved wife died. He explains their relationship this way: "It had reached its proper perfection. This had become what it had in it to be. Therefore of course it could not be prolonged. As if God said, Good, you have mastered that exercise.

I am very pleased with it. And now you are ready to go on to the next."

My marriage and family with Jason had come to its fulfillment—its perfection. It was exactly as God had intended it to be during those ten years I was blessed to spend with him. We, as a couple, accomplished our part of the grander story, and then it reached its proper perfection and could be no more. There were no more scenes for the two of us to enact because the curtain had fallen on our life together. He ran his race and won his crown of life. I have a difficult time imagining myself with him in the present, as I've changed and evolved, and in many ways, it doesn't seem like we would fit very well anymore—and that might be true because he's been in the presence of the Almighty. He's received his standing ovation, and I haven't yet, but I hope to one day. I'm still here, in a new act, with a new leading man. Ryan was meant for these years—however long they may be (until we're old and gray, I pray). My eight children were meant for this act. It's all part of a grander plan that I have come to accept and trust.

I will always ache when I think about those difficult years and the pain they ushered into my life, just as I will ache for my unborn baby, but there is also a peace in the present. I don't yearn for what *was* because those thoughts are a waste of time and energy. I look forward—not behind.

We have seven children who have lost a parent—that's a painful experience to have at such a young age. There will be a yearning and a grief that they will always have, but we explain that they can either wallow in grief in what is lost or rejoice in what they have gained. It's a choice. To live in regret or to move forward in thanksgiving.

Having gone through so much heartache as a family, we reach out when we see someone hurting over the death of a loved one or experiencing other unforeseen tragedies. Even if it's saying, "I have no idea what to say"—those words are lifegiving and truly acknowledge a person's suffering. We try to offer something tangible as well—lawn care, laundry, babysitting, or a meal—and even if they say they are fine, the gesture is always appreciated.

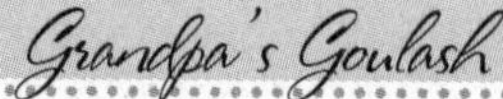

This is my go-to meal to bring a family in need. The simple flavors develop over time as it slowly simmers in a Crock-Pot or on the back burner of the stove, and who doesn't love a good goulash? It goes great with the healthy cornbread recipe from Chapter Two.

- 1 pound of lean ground beef or ground turkey
- A bag of spinach (my own addition to Grandpa's original recipe)
- 10–15 mushrooms, diced
- 1 large yellow onion, diced
- 3 large cloves of garlic, finely minced
- 2 14.5-ounce cans of diced tomatoes with juice
- 2 15-ounce cans of tomato sauce
- Salt and pepper to taste
- 2 tsp Italian seasoning
- 2 cups cooked small elbow macaroni
- 1 cup (or more to taste) of shredded mozzarella cheese or nutritional yeast

Preheat the oven to 350 degrees. Heat a Dutch oven on the stove and then add the ground beef or turkey, onion, and garlic. Cook, stirring occasionally, until browned. Add the mushrooms and spinach. Cook until the spinach is wilted. Spoon off some of the excess fat. Add the remaining ingredients and simmer on low for about 20 minutes. Stir occasionally. Stir in the macaroni noodles and simmer for five minutes. Top with cheese or nutritional yeast. Cover with foil and pop in the oven until the cheese melts—about 15–20 minutes. Share with a friend in need or treat your family to a hearty feast!

Returning to Savannah: On Facing Disappointment and Choosing Faith

I have a complicated history with Savannah, Georgia, full of love, joy, pain, and failed expectations.

Ryan and I met in Savannah in 2010—approximately two months after our introduction online. After weeks of emails, texts, and phone calls, we hesitantly decided that it was time to meet in person. We also decided that the initial meeting could not occur in either of our home states. Until we knew that the relationship was moving forward, we wanted to protect the kids, and so we settled on Savannah: a place of beauty and warmth, and one that neither of us had visited.

I scheduled various people to watch Caleb, Lucas, Mabel, and Josh as I prepared to meet a stranger I had admittedly fallen in love with over the course of a few weeks. A man I had never officially met, as strange as it all sounds. The rest was history.

Our weekend together was wonderful, filled with love and romance, and as I boarded the plane home from the Savannah airport, my phone buzzed with a text from Ryan: *I love you Jess and can't wait to spend the rest of my life with you.*

Four years later, now married, I would awaken on my thirty-seventh birthday to another text from Ryan: *Jess, pack your bags, we're returning to Savannah.*

I was elated! We were going back to a place I loved. Going back after the miscarriage. Going back with the green light to try again. Going back with high expectations.

I had felt slightly nauseous the week prior to leaving and was anxiously awaiting the right time to take another pregnancy test. We lost our baby in December, and the miscarriage process had been long and painful, as my body refused to completely let go of the remains. I finally agreed to a D&C procedure three months later, in March. My body had been slowly healing over the past five weeks, and the doctor reassured us there was no reason we couldn't try again if we were emotionally ready. He did mention that it would be best to wait one menstrual cycle, but it wasn't necessary. I'm not one to wait for anything, being the least patient person on the planet, and so we did not proceed with caution. We got right back into the swing of things and now—on my thirty-seventh birthday—I was feeling nauseous, which was the best present I could have ever asked for! And how romantic that we were traveling to Savannah, the place where we met, where I hoped we would find out we were pregnant again.

Wow! I thought. *God is so cool in how he worked out the romantic details.* And, knowing how God worked, I was convinced that this baby would be a girl and then we'd name her Savannah, of course.

We drove ten hours in eager anticipation. Ryan knew I was convinced I was pregnant, and although he was slightly apprehensive about getting his hopes up, he was also excited about the possibility of discovering our good news in Savannah.

We located our hotel (the same hotel we had stayed in the first time we had met), entered the same elevator, and began kissing, reliving the magic from the first time around.

My nausea continued to intensify when we entered our room, and then I began cramping. Feeling light-headed and woozy, I turned to Ryan and said, "I need to lay down for a minute. I'm not feeling so great."

I sprawled out on the king-size bed and held my belly. The cramps were severe, but I assumed it was the baby implanting into my uterus—of course it was, because that's how the plan had to unfold. God wouldn't bring us to this beautiful city, where we had met and fallen in love, for any other reason, would he?

Ryan laid beside me and held my hand—unsure of what to do or say as I moaned and complained of nausea. So far, the romance factor wasn't very promising. I got up to use the bathroom.

The sight I saw crushed me. Blood. There was no baby and there would be no romance on this surprise vacation. Tears seeped out of the corners of my eyes as my expectations were flushed down the toilet.

My first post-miscarriage menstrual cycle had begun with the worst timing ever. Not only had my period arrived, but I had read that the first post-miscarriage one was usually the worst and characterized by heavy bleeding, nausea, and cramping as the body figures out how to get back on track.

I exited the bathroom and shared the disappointing news with Ryan. He held me and reassured me that a pregnancy would happen when it was supposed to, and although I knew there was truth in his words, it was a hard reality to swallow.

Our romantic weekend didn't turn out to be romantic in the traditional sense, but it was meaningful in how Ryan cared for my heart and body. He ministered loving truth to me as I questioned and wailed against God's will for our life and indulged me with back rubs, holding me as I wept.

I can't imagine a place that represents more pleasure or pain than Savannah does, which is interesting because, when I think about it, my marriage is a lot like this romantic town. What Ryan and I have is beautiful, like Savannah, which drips of historical beauty with cobblestone roads, quaint cafes, and creeping vines everywhere. We brought history, children, and baggage to our relationship, but in that history, there was depth and beauty; however, we also cause each other pleasure and pain—sometimes on the same day—but this doesn't detract from the overall beauty of what we have.

We will always have pleasure and pain in this life of ours—met and unmet expectations—but we can't limit ourselves to those descriptions. We need to recognize the bigger story, the overall beauty of our God-ordained partnership. Not denying the pain but accepting it as part of a package that also includes joy.

TAKEAWAYS

- Don't be a drama queen like me. Truly, my overactive imagination can get the best of me at times as I convince myself that life has to happen in a specific series of steps, and in doing so, I put God in a very limited box. You would think by now I would know better.
- Step away from the immediate situation and try to see the bigger picture of what the Lord may be saying or teaching. It's not always easy, but I've found that if I ask for wisdom, he is faithful to provide it; however, this prayer may be answered in the form of having a sense of peace instead of having all the answers.
- Find comfort in your spouse. Our spouses are a gift, and they are supposed to be a source of comfort as we walk through difficult times. I know many women have a difficult time accepting comfort from their husbands, but it is a gift you can also give him as you allow him to wrap his arms around you.

English 666: Encouraging One Another through Difficult Times

I started a master's degree program in 2004, the year of Lucas's birth. I dreamt of being a college professor, and obtaining an advanced degree in English was a requirement for this position.

This particular program required thirty credits, which had to be completed in ten years. *No problem*, I thought. It's funny how fast ten years flies by with pregnancies, babies, special needs, cancer, remarriage, and seven children. I woke up one day, and it was 2011! I only had three remaining years to complete this degree, and I was only halfway done! The outstanding requirements included five classes, so I immediately signed up for a night option in our first year of marital bliss. That was followed by a day class the following semester, and then I took 2012 completely off as we settled into our blended life. The year 2013 brought an unexpected move to rural Tennessee, and I had three remaining classes. This was also the year I experienced a miscarriage but still desired a baby. My to-do list was growing.

I decided to get creative. I emailed my advisor, told her my story, and she agreed to a yearlong extension that included an independent study worth six credits, but I still needed one last class. I researched online and chose the University of Kentucky, which offered upper-level courses that could be transferred to my graduate program. I immediately enrolled in the only class with availability, ENG 666: Feministic Literature. The 666 should have been a sign to steer clear, but desperate times call for desperate measures. The professor did not appreciate my tendency toward sarcasm or witty banter. She also didn't give two hoots that I had seven children and was pregnant with an eighth. In fact, this only seemed to ignite her passion for making me prove my worth in academia. I would not receive any grace with her presiding over my future. She and I did not share the same worldview, the same faith, or the same vision for moving through life, and she displayed her lack of affection by awarding me with consistently low grades. A grade of a B or higher was required in order to transfer this class into my program, and it seemed like a very attainable goal, since I had never in my life earned anything lower than a B!

I bounced out of bed the morning that final grades were posted and ran to check online. My final grade was a B–. I emailed the professor and begged for extra credit, explaining how this was the last class I had to take for my program, but the grade remained. She would not offer me any mercy. I had one remaining semester before the clock ran out, the spring of 2015, and I had to take one final class in order to graduate within the parameters of the extension. I was simply over the whole endeavor. One class to go, and I was ready to throw in the towel after eleven years.

Ryan awoke to find me sitting on the porch, wiping away tears.

"I got a B–. I'm finished," I said while stroking the growing baby within my belly.

He looked at me and said: "You're not done. You have come this far, and you will never forgive yourself if you don't suck it up and finish. Take the weekend to decompress and then get on the phone with your advisor Monday morning and wrap this up. You are graduating in April."

I took my husband's advice and emailed my advisor, and she offered mercy! She suggested a final independent study course—a course I had complete liberty to create! The requirement was to read five books and write essays on each one. Five books of my choosing. I couldn't ask for a better course for the reader/writer in me. Three months later, I received my grade—an A.

I walked across the stage at Grand Valley State University to accept my master's degree eleven years after I had started and seven months pregnant because my husband wouldn't let me quit and instead encouraged me to keep going. Keep persevering. He encouraged me to keep moving forward, simply doing the next thing that I had to do.

Life can be overwhelmingly difficult at times—especially blended life. You may be two years in, eleven years in, or even twenty-five years in, and I'm sure there are times when a lack of mercy or grace or understanding has caused one of you or maybe both to consider throwing in the towel. Let me suggest this instead—offer grace. When your spouse isn't seeing potential or isn't being merciful, extend grace anyway. When your stepchild only sees the negative, offer mercy. Hold on until the page flips—and it usually does. When one of you doesn't know how to move forward anymore, then step up and offer encouragement. Life is hard and God is good—but not in the way that the world likes to throw that saying around. No, it doesn't always feel good in the moments or the weeks or maybe the months, but hold on and make those tiny steps toward change: encouragement rather than disdain, grace instead of suspicion, mercy when actions require swift punishment, joy traded for anger. Slowly but surely, nine times out of ten, change will occur.

And take ownership of your part in the chaos. Personally, I felt like that professor had it out for me, but maybe I wasn't accomplishing work worthy of an A or even a B. I was exhausted and pregnant, and maybe she was justified in giving me that grade. And I could have absolutely been justified in quitting altogether. Instead, I got creative (with my husband's encouragement). I found a tiny bit of strength to persevere, and I graduated. I did it. My seven children saw their mom walk across the stage to accept a diploma that took eleven years to obtain, which then led to my dream job as a college professor.

Thank you, Ryan, for always believing in me.

Annabelle Ryan: Embracing Change by Going with the Flow

It took three months for my body to let go of our first baby. Then came the D&C and then healing from the D&C. And there was an additional six-month attempt to become pregnant with Annabelle, despite my best efforts to control the situation with every natural pregnancy remedy known to mankind.

When I finally saw those two pink lines, very faint after the day my period was supposed to begin, I had to confirm it with six more sticks—just to make sure I was actually pregnant.

The sticks didn't lie. Disbelief and fear intermingled with excitement as I exited the bathroom to find Ryan: "Honey, honey . . . ." My voice quivered as I ushered him into the bathroom to gaze upon the beautiful lineup of pregnancy sticks on top of the toilet. He smiled and exclaimed, "That's great, babe," in his calm, Ryan-like way.

"Why aren't you more excited?!" I questioned.

"I am excited," he replied. "I don't show it, but I'm jumping up and down inside."

But I didn't care. He could celebrate in his own dud way. I was grinning from ear to ear and literally jumping up and down until I realized this might harm the new life growing inside of me, so I stopped.

Both of us were hesitant about getting too excited, in case something tragic reoccurred. I tend to fear the worst-case scenario because it has happened numerous times. My child was born with profound special needs. My husband did die. Ryan's wife died. And we lost a baby. Worst-case scenarios aren't uncommon in and around my life. I nervously embraced joy, but I more enthusiastically embraced fear. Fear, unfortunately, controlled me for the remainder of that pregnancy.

I went through at least twenty pregnancy sticks over the next week, and the lines continued to darken. (Thank goodness Amazon sells them in bulk.). Then the reality of pregnancy sank in.

Weeks five, six, and seven were right on track as the nausea began and the sight of meat and almost anything that didn't include saltine crackers sent me running to the toilet, gagging.

Then came the dreaded eighth week. I woke up feeling decent, just as I had with the other pregnancy, and my heart sank.

Oh God, no, no, no, no, no. Please, not again.

I pleaded and pleaded.

I frantically called the doctor, who scheduled me for an afternoon visit. Ryan stopped working and drove me to Jackson, Tennessee, ninety miles away. My body shook like a leaf as I walked through the revolving doors, and I couldn't meet the eyes of any of the pregnant women in the waiting room. I sat down in a gray, padded chair and focused on the blue specks in the tile in front of me, kicking a gum wrapper around with my foot to pass the time and give the impression of nonchalance.

The nurse peeked her head through the door and called out, "Jessica!"

I blindly rose, steadied by Ryan's arm, and followed her into the examination room. I lay on the vinyl table as the nurse retrieved her Doppler. Up and down my belly she went, searching for a heartbeat but finding only silence. I lay there perfectly still, not daring to breathe, lest my breath overshadow the distant sound of a tiny heartbeat. I stared straight into Ryan's eyes as the tears began to sneak past my firm resolve—*drip, drip, drip.* One minute, two minutes—*tick, tick, tick* bellowed the clock on the wall, signaling life's movement forward at its rawest, realest moments. Signaling that time will wait for no one. It marches on through our pain, and we must eventually succumb to its will and find the strength to live again or be left behind to wallow in despair.

Why do I have a nurse? I began to wonder, questioning the competence of someone who might not have a medical degree. *Maybe she's still in school and doesn't know what she's looking for. Why isn't the doctor here? I'm an at-risk patient. With my history and advanced age, I shouldn't have an aid or a nurse looking for the heartbeat . . .*

Tick, tick, tick.

Drip, drip, drip.

The clock and my tears marched on.

Fearful thoughts blanketed any rationality that might remain. And then *tick, tick, tick* was replaced with a faint *thump, thump, thump.*

"There it is!" she joyfully exclaimed. "Little bugger was hard to find!"

I exhaled and the tears stopped their meticulous march forward.

The Doppler lady had just become my new best friend.

I left that day filled with hope but wasn't able to leave my anxiety behind. I spent the next six months anxiously monitoring every detail of that pregnancy. I bought a personal Doppler to check the baby on an hourly, sometimes every ten-minute, basis. I monitored kicks and thumps and the heartbeat until the day of delivery. I had numerous appointments because of my high-risk status and iron issues that caused me to devour red meat and onions—even requesting an overabundance of them when Ryan and I frequented our normal date-night spot.

"This is a strange request," I would preface to the unsuspecting waitress. "Could you add extra onions on that French dip? And maybe a side of onions too?"

As we neared the end of the pregnancy, the doctor suggested a special ultrasound that would determine any problems we might encounter when the baby was delivered. We declined. We had gotten through the twenty-week ultrasound with flying colors—the ultrasound where I had heard the news about Lucas and the ultrasound that put me on edge for weeks prior to its occurrence. Finally, we were in the home stretch. It was only one week until we would meet our baby.

June 12, 2015. Ryan and I spent the night at a hotel in preparation for an early morning C-section. The experience was very different with this delivery than it had been with my other four. I don't know if it was due to my age or the geographical difference, but if something could have gone wrong, it did.

The spinal tap wouldn't go in. Ryan almost fainted and had to leave the room. I began to cry in agony when the doctor made the incision because the spinal tap hadn't completely taken effect. Annabelle came out of my womb purple with the cord around her neck, and as I held my newborn baby, elated with her beauty and God's faithfulness, a frantic nurse took one look at me, pale as a ghost, and ran out of the room to find the doctor.

That's when I began to bleed out. My arms went limp as I encouraged my new daughter to nurse.

The next few hours were a blur and required a frantic blood transfusion. When we arrived home, an immense amount of patience was required as I regained my strength, and Ryan took the reins of home life with the other kids. Yes, it was worth it, but through the process, we learned that flexibility is an absolute must, and instead of fretting about what next week or next month might bring, we need to focus on each moment as it arrives. Moment by moment. Step by step. That's how God's faithfulness shows up in our lives.

And Annabelle, good golly. She just turned five at the time of this writing, and has been an absolute joy and a perfect final addition. Annabelle has taught me that I really can go years without sleeping. She has her siblings wrapped around her little finger (especially her big brother Tate) and serves as the glue to truly strengthen the blended bond in our family. I'm incredibly thankful that I didn't allow fear to keep me from one of the greatest joys of my life—being her old mom.

Just like her bright and sunny personality, Annabelle's favorite food is easy as pie—pizza pie! We love making homemade pizza in our outdoor pizza oven, and this tradition has led to Annabelle excitedly exclaiming, "Pizza is my *favorite* food!"

After years of experimentation, I think I've finally perfected the art of the perfect pizza crust. I hope you love it as much as we do.

- 1½ tsp active dry yeast
- 1½ tsp sea salt
- 4 cups of bread flour
- 1 cup of whole wheat flour
- 2–2½ cups of filtered water
- 2 tbsp apple cider vinegar

Mix the flours, yeast, and sea salt in a large bowl. Slowly add the vinegar and water, increasing the water by 1/2 cup intervals. You do not want the dough to be too wet or too dry! This is a very fine balance. Knead for about 7 minutes until the dough is nice and elastic. Place it in an oiled bowl and let it rise. This dough is really good if it's used the day it's made, but the flavors develop into amazingness if it's allowed to develop and mature in the fridge for a few days prior to use. Top with sauce and your favorite ingredients, and either bake in a pizza oven or on a pizza stone at 500 degrees for about 10 minutes. (Keep an eye on it!)

7

YOURS, MINE, AND OURS

Perseverance in Parenting

I once overheard a conversation one of my children was having with an older couple. They were talking about our life, their siblings, and how fun it is to be a part of a big family, and then the woman turned to my child and asked, "Who are your *real* brothers and sisters?"

My child responded with the biological names.

Then the woman said, "Is that your real dad or your real mom?"

My tongue began to throb as I bit down on it.

A year into marriage, Ryan and I finalized the adoption of each other's biological children because we didn't want our kids to feel as if some of them were *real* to one parent and others were not real, and we've done a good job of eliminating these labels. We have never allowed a pick-and-choose buffet when it comes to our family, and this boundary includes extended family members. It was always an *accept all or none* understanding, and everyone has responded respectfully to this desire. Our children usually feel confident in their blended identity, until outsiders ask ignorant questions, which then produces the undesired result of making them doubt themselves and who they are in our family unit.

The definition of *real* is this: being an actual thing, having objective existence, and not being imaginary. We are a *real* family. We have an objective existence, which is not imaginary. We are not a stepfamily. We are a blended family. We take real ownership of what we are and what we are not. We don't pretend that I gave birth to eight children, but I am the real, active mom to each child, and Ryan is the real, active dad.

Questions like those posited by the older couple, although asked without malice and probably in ignorance, are not appropriate. Not only are they inappropriate, but they have the potential to be extremely hurtful and often have the additional tendency to imply that the children are not part of a real family situation. Instead, the implication suggests, it was their unfortunate luck to get a *fake* family. These questions also enable the construction of boundaries (real or imaginary) between biological and adopted members, as our kids question their identity and place within this perceived unreal family situation. Children in situations such as ours, or adoptive children in general, already have questions about identity, where they fit in the world, and their place in the family. They also tend to harbor doubts about the structure and security of their new family unit, and these feelings shouldn't be amplified by strangers.

Ryan's Take

I grew up in a blended family. My mom and dad divorced when I was young, and my mom remarried when I was fourteen. Stewart, the man she married, was my stepdad and has always been that to me. My biological father, although absent, was still my dad. Stewart had two children from his previous marriage, and he and my mom had a son together. Even then, when I introduced his children, it was always "This is my little brother and sister." I needed them to know they were accepted into the family—a lesson I already understood even as a young teenager. Jess and I have instilled this same basic principle into our blended family. I have to admit, I was initially hesitant about her blood children taking my last name. Not because I didn't want them to carry on my name; it was more about respect to their bloodline and carrying on their given name. After a long evaluation, we decided it was more important in our situation with young children to become one family and all share the same name, to ensure that no one felt different or left out. After nearly ten years, I realize it was the right decision for us. We have eight kids, period. I'm not "Stepdad" and Jess is not "Stepmom," and neither of us has any "stepchildren." It doesn't detract from their birth parents, but instead allows us to feel like a family, in the here and now, which is what is really important. We're blended, yes, but still united as one. If you ever ask one of our kids to introduce Jess and me or any one of their siblings, they will sound like I did as a young teen: "This is my brother, sister, mom, and dad." Exactly how we want them to feel—like they are part of a real family.

The name game can be a sensitive issue for our family and for families like ours. Our children have one earthly mom and one earthly dad. We acknowledge that there was another parent, a parent who loved them fiercely, but our faith tells us that he or she is in heaven, where there are no longer any parenting duties.

Neither deceased parent plays an active role in raising these children, and are referred to as Mom or Dad in heaven. Ryan and I are the God-appointed, active, and engaged parents—the *only* active parents. No one is subbing in, we don't have every other weekend to ourselves, and we don't get breaks. We are two people who try day in and day out to be the best we can possibly be for our eight children. To suggest that someone is not a real mom or a real dad is hurtful, especially when we participate in all the real aspects of parenting, such as discipline, family meetings, devotions, driving to and from practices and school, cooking, lazy-river days, laying out school clothes, haircuts, snuggles, heart-to-heart talks, tears and laughter, screen-time talks, eye rolls, and the list could go on and on because a parent's to-do list is never complete—especially two parents who don't get time off!

We do the *real work* of raising *real kids*, so that makes us *real parents*, and we might even have the opportunity to contribute a positive trait or two to their lives occasionally. Just maybe.

TAKEAWAYS

- As an outsider, consider that it might not be your place to ask the specifics about a family situation—especially if you don't know the family very well.
- If you have a curiosity that simply cannot be shaken about the biological members of a family unit, be sure to present the question in a respectful way. And *please* be careful about asking when the kids are present. Unless I'm heavily pressed, I won't differentiate between my biological children and the adopted ones in the presence of my kids. It's happened before, and I didn't like the looks of quiet, almost shame-like shadows that crossed

their faces, suggesting that they weren't as good as nor as wanted as their siblings who are biologically mine.

- It's important to set boundaries for your blended family. You are allowed to say, "I'm not comfortable discussing this topic right now." Period. You are especially allowed to say this if the topic being discussed is going to hurt your children in any way. Period.
- Always remember to come back to grace. Our heavenly Father pours out his grace upon our ignorance and stupid decisions and inappropriate questions, and we should extend the same to those who know not what they do. Usually a respectful but firm explanation goes a long way. And when all else fails—grace.

Nature versus Nurture: Accepting Our Children and Celebrating Their Uniqueness

There's the age-old argument, "Is it nature or nurture?" For whatever reason, human beings need an explanation for everything, even down to why a child acts a certain way or displays specific tendencies. I believe it's a little of both. My adopted children, Tate, Mya, and Jada, share certain behaviors and traits, and my biological children, Caleb, Lucas, Mabel, and Josh, also do. The jury is still out on Annabelle. Will she lean to the left and be a lingerer, enthusiastic, and want more out of life than life can ever give? Will she savor the foods she loves, licking a piece of fudge slowly like a sucker and making it last all day? (That's a special kind of talent.) Will she prefer to play outside, expending her inexhaustible energy on outdoor fun: swimming, running, playing tag, or building forts? Will she moan and groan for more every single time, never satisfied with what she's been given? Will she eat from my spoon and not be disgusted? Or will she recoil at the thought? Will she be like Ryan's biological kids, throwing caution to the wind? Or will she lean to the right and overthink every decision to death? Will she ponder the potential consequences of her actions before acting? Will she never get overly excited about anything? Will she be even tempered? Will she be suspicious when Mom and Dad suggest that there's a surprise waiting for her? Will she be not quite sure about anything or anyone until they earn her trust? Will she be efficient and dependable? Eating for nutrition rather than for enjoyment? Choosing to play outside for a little bit but then returning to a quiet oasis inside to rest? Will she lean in one direction over the other? Or will she be a blend? Completing her chores without being told like Caleb and Mya? Or needing glasses like Tate and Mabel and sharing her vast opinions, which are always correct, on everything? Will she align herself with the babies, Josh and Jada, who require constant reminders? Will she be musically inclined like Caleb? Or enjoy reading like Josh and Mya? Numerous possibilities. So many potential traits. Maybe she'll blaze her own Annabelle-unique trail. Only time will tell, I suppose.

There is truth in nature, and there is truth in nurture. Each set of children with similar genetic makeups displays similar tendencies—there is absolutely no denying this fact. But Ryan and I have also had a hand in molding our kids as individuals. Caleb loves to fish and was taught this skill by Ryan, his adopted dad, who also loves to fish. Jason hated fishing. Caleb is also a gifted guitar player—a skill he was introduced to while living in Tennessee, a state Ryan and I moved him to. If Jason had continued to be the primary father figure in Caleb's life, Caleb probably would not have developed a love for fishing or playing guitar, and would have instead been introduced to activities such as tennis or golf—two of Jason's passions. Maybe fishing and music would have found their way into his life through different avenues, but more likely, they would not have.

Mya loves to craft and crochet and bake—three hobbies I introduced her to. She also has a heart for the special-needs community, via the exposure she's gleaned through being Lucas's sister and experiences she probably wouldn't have had without him as a brother.

Ryan's Take

I really love kids. Broad statement, but it's true, and I am especially fond of babies. I am also usually very adaptable, and in some cases, that's a positive trait, especially as a father who decided to adopt four children all at once! However, that being said, adding Lucas to my fatherhood quiver was not something I was prepared for. I am one of those hands-on dads and try to do my part changing diapers and cleaning up throw-up and all the other unmentionables that are created by young children, but here I am now, ten years into family life with Jess, and I thought those stages would be long over. It took a few years for the reality to sink in that these stages will probably never end with Lucas. When I first met him, Jess and I had just started dating, and we were at her house when Lucas started hollering, "Daddy!" When we went into his room together and I met him, he calmed for a second and really looked me over and started again: "Daddy, Daddy, Daddy." It broke my heart, and he's had it ever since. Like most men, I love a good underdog story, and Lucas has the best story. He has truly earned the right to not only live and breathe but thrive like few have with his diagnosis. Don't get me wrong, changing a sixteen-year-old's diapers is not fun, and his screaming can bring me to my knees, but he is my son, and I will fight for him until one of us breathes our last. I have witnessed his will to survive. When he had shunt complications and ended up in the ICU for nearly six weeks, I was his roommate. Jess drew the short straw and had to stay at home with the other seven kids. I watched as they tried to keep him sedated and silently laughed when the latest nurse would stand next to him and declare she would give him what he needed to keep him still, only to jump out of her skin as he sat up in bed and pulled at his tubes. Even fully sedated, he couldn't be restrained from fighting his way through the fog. I watched his heart rate decrease when I would talk, calming him enough to bring him back to a normal rhythm. I have learned so much from his desire to live and to accept things that are out of my control and embrace what God has given me. He doesn't sit and dwell on his bad fortune. He is my son and I am his dad and in his case, he doesn't know any other way. I have gladly accepted the baton that was passed down and love all eight of our kids, with all of their differing personalities. I understand some of them better than others, but I know that's not any reflection of the blended nature of our family but more so simply personality differences. Blood or not, we are sharing life together, and I wouldn't want it any other way.

Parenting is a lot like mining. We enter the mine shaft with our child, chipping away as we unearth different talents and passions, every once in a while discovering what we think is a true gem, a true passion, but the excitement fizzles as we discover it's only fool's gold and not worth pursuing. But we keep mining, keep getting in there with each child, unearthing passions and talents—either from a genetic makeup that they received at birth or exposure that we may have gifted them with. Does it matter in the end? There's this idea that a deceased parent will always be with a child, and maybe this is true (I'm not sure), but I believe the experience of losing someone we love is more like lighting a beautiful scented candle. We light the candle, and it slowly burns throughout the day, leaving behind the essence of lavender or vanilla wafting through the air, and then the day turns to night, and as we head to bed, we blow out the flame. The fragrant smell lingers but eventually diminishes and disappears altogether. That was my experience with Jason's death. His scent lingered for weeks, with the essence of who he was as a man, as a person, seen in the mundane every day, like his toothbrush beside the sink and his shoes that were never worn again but evenly displayed in the hallway. Eventually, as I moved forward and began to live again, the scent faded as the belongings found new homes, and my memories became fuzzy and sometimes unreliable. My ten years of life beside Jason will never be erased, and these memories have absolutely shaped the woman I am today. As did living with my parents for eighteen years. As did my college experiences and those relationships. Seven of my kids have the genetic makeup of another person who is no longer in their life—his or her mannerisms, talents, desires, and flaws—and we see this evidence as they grow and mature. Their experiences with Jason or Kaci will shape who they are as individuals and who they become, but they are also being shaped and taught by a new parent—exposed to new ideas, concepts, and ways of approaching life. They are being shaped by every person they encounter in life! Teachers, friends, friends' parents, relatives—every individual becomes an opportunity for growth and exploration. The more positive influences in anyone's life, the better chance they have of becoming healthy, productive, and respectful members of society, and isn't this what we all desire for our children (both those with our genetic makeup and those without)?

Speaking of children without our genetic makeup—there might be that one child who is simply difficult to connect with or get along with, and the grace is lacking because there is no biological connection. Maybe this child has unresolved anger or guilt? Maybe there's confusion or pain because they were thrown into a new life? Maybe it's simply a clash of personalities? I've had this child, too, and I can honestly say that time and patience were my allies, as I experienced years of guilt, questioning my role in his life.

That Kid: Bonding with a Child Who Makes It Difficult

When two families come together, there are two cultures that immediately need to mesh—two ways of doing life and two sets of normal. Sometimes these sets closely align, and this makes the process much easier, and sometimes these two sets do not align, which can lead to a unique set of challenges. Successful blending requires patience and time as different personalities, coping mechanisms, and behaviors come together. In our situation, one parent was used to a normal that included quiet, introverted children, and this parent was also very introverted herself, but with the blending of the new family, she suddenly found herself raising the most talkative, argumentative, inquisitive, and quite-possibly-up-for-presidential-election-someday kid, Tate Riley Ronne.

Oh, my goodness. Tate is amazing. He also never backs down from a challenge, an argument, has never known a stranger, and when I was first introduced to him, he never stopped talking. This is a child whose biological grandfather balked at driving him to school anymore because of all the nonstop talking. This is the child whose biological grandmother quietly expressed concern when I became his mom: "I wonder how Jess is going to respond to all of Tate's chattiness?"

I was also worried about how Caleb was going to respond to Tate's extroverted nature, as Caleb is naturally quiet and withdrawn, but his new brother didn't seem to ruffle his feathers like they ruffled mine.

Tate and I were introduced when he was seven. He was the life of all the parties, and he never stopped talking. Have I mentioned this already? If he felt like I was fleeing the scene because I was overwhelmed (which I often did in those early years, seeking solitude wherever I could), he felt the need to make things better by talking, by offering an explanation or a reason for the behavior—which is how he would feel better as an extrovert. If I was in a contemplative mood or enjoying a moment of peace, he felt the need to fill the silence because, in his mind, silence was bad. You help people by talking to them so that they don't have to experience the sad, bad silence, and as much as I tried to avoid feeling overwhelmed, Tate's never-ending excitability wore me out. I wasn't used to one child needing so much of my mental space, and I resented that most of my words were used on him. I found myself often hiding in the bathtub to reenergize (which was becoming a multiple-times-a-day habit). Tate was sucking the life out of me, and I wasn't sure how to improve the situation without hurting my relationship with him. I often bemoaned to Ryan about my dilemma behind closed doors.

"Tate follows me around all day, talking and talking and talking!" I would wail.

The response I got?

"Don't worry about it. He'll eventually outgrow it. I was just like him."

What? I married a Tate! I was floored. How could my husband have been like Tate as a child?

When I have a problem, I research the heck out of it until I find an answer, and I tackled this particular personality clash with the same level of diligence that I had applied to many of my problems in the past—with a good old-fashioned Google search. I typed "differences between extroverts and introverts" and stumbled across an eye-opening blog post, exhaling in relief as I read it. The author discussed the subtle and not-so-subtle differences between personalities—how introverted people are drained with socialization and extroverted people are fueled by people and words. As I continued to compile research and pore over blog posts, I realized how introverted I was, how introverted many of my children were, and how extremely extroverted Tate was. Neither of us did anything wrong in being who we were created to be, but moving forward, we needed to better understand our differences in order to peacefully coexist. I presented this newfound information at the dinner table, speaking in generalizations about introverted and extroverted personalities and how they differ, rather than signaling out Tate specifically.

But, being the smart kid that he is, he caught on quickly, exclaiming midconversation, "That's why you and Caleb like to be alone in your rooms sometimes! You're recharging!" Ding! Ding! Ding! We have a winner! It clicked!

We had a healthy, informative conversation that night about our individual differences and how we could work together to be more respectful of an introvert's need for solitude and an extrovert's need for socialization.

As Tate has matured, his talkative nature has wound down considerably—just like his father told me it would. There's something in his nature that I'm really drawn to—just like his father. He has an amazing ability to present an argument in a coherent, respectful way, and everyone enjoys being around him. He's a magnet who draws people in with his charisma and charm. I know God has a great plan for his life in some capacity. (I would wager in politics or law.)

Maybe you have this kid too. Believe me, I know how exhausting it can be! Especially when everything in you wants to have a healthy, happy relationship with your children. Kids have an amazing capacity to understand—much more so than we give them credit for. Tate had a lightbulb moment as I was explaining the differences in personalities. I think as mothers we often suffer from the martyr syndrome, and this goes so far as to make us avoid what we would perceive to be difficult conversations. I was nervous about bringing up our differences, but Tate understood, and the conversation changed the entire trajectory of our life together—for the better. Sometimes it's as simple as a conversation, and sometimes it's more like therapy. Only you can answer what's appropriate for your situation, but I would encourage you to take the steps needed to improve whatever relationship may be hurting in your family.

Tate can eat sloppy joes like he can talk—lots and lots and lots—and these are super easy to make and only improve with time as the flavors meld together on the back of the stove. You can use ground turkey, ground hamburger, ground venison, or a combination, for a delicious meal to keep even the most talkative of mouths full—momentarily, that is.

- 3 pounds of meat (your choice—ground turkey, hamburger, or venison)
- ¼ cup apple cider vinegar
- 3 tbsp Worcestershire sauce
- 3-4 tbsp maple syrup (adjust to taste)
- 3-4 cups ketchup
- Salt and pepper to taste

Fry the meat, and drain the oil. Return the meat to the pan. Add the remaining ingredients and slowly simmer for about 30 minutes. Stir occasionally. Pile high on hamburger buns.

Go Play! Persevering through the Difficult Years of Parenthood

I shooed one of my children out of the kitchen, annoyance growing by the minute with yet another complaint of boredom or a long-winded tale about how one sibling had grossly mistreated another. It sure felt like we were on day 100 million of this year's particularly long winter break, which marched on and on and on with the recent bout of inclement weather and now influenza circulating throughout the schools.

Ahhh, good times.

I sighed, frustrated at how much energy the kids required during these days without school and irritated with the constant boredom. We had purchased a beautiful property in the middle of rural Tennessee on thirty acres of land, a mighty river flowing in our backyard, with the expectation that our children would spend their days romping through the fields, building forts, playing tag and hide-and-seek, plucking fresh fruit from the apple and pear trees, and whatever else they were able to convince one another to play or do, but that wasn't generally the case. Usually, they were inside the house, bellyaching about how bored they were.

I returned my attention to the pot on the back burner of the stove, which held dinner for the evening. I began to stir, slowly encouraging the flavors of a simmering beef stroganoff to meld together, an easy family favorite consisting of hamburger, chopped onions, garlic, and mushrooms drenched in a cream-cheese sauce. I inhaled the savory aroma as music played in the background. "I'll praise you in this storm," belted out an old-time favorite by the popular group Casting Crowns.

I'd been experiencing a bit of a faith crisis in the recent months as I desperately grasped for control while life spiraled further away from me. So many balls were in the air. The hormonal issues that inevitably arrive with aging. Teaching, which I loved but didn't love as much as writing. Writing, which was my passion but doesn't really pay the bills—at least not yet. Raising eight children, now with several teenagers and a toddler. Struggling to do right by Lucas, in pursuit of the best options for him but also needing to sacrifice more of our limited resources and time. The list went on.

It felt overwhelming 90 percent of the time, and I knew I wasn't handling the demands well. Most of my prayers were more like complaints and resembled grumbling as I begged for superhuman strength to get through the days—annoyed that God would bequeath so many responsibilities upon my weary, aging shoulders.

"Praise you in this storm, huh?" I muttered. I had fiercely believed those words during the most difficult days of life—as a baby grew in my belly in 2004 (a child proclaimed terminal even before taking his first breath) and again as my husband Jason took his last breath here on earth. Now, in my current reality, with a healthy family, a good marriage, my daily needs met, I couldn't seem to muster up any praise in this pathetic little pity party of a storm I was having for myself.

Jesus, help . . . , I sighed in resignation and frustration.

Go play, I heard gently whispered in reply.

What? I wondered.

Go play! Stop complaining and stop focusing on the negative, and stop stressing about everything that I ultimately control, and stop the bellyaching, and go play! Enjoy the life I made for you! Bask in my creation, jump on the trampoline with your kids, breathe in the beauty of nature all around, enjoy your life, enjoy what I have created for you—for your pleasure! Take joy in the food you are preparing, savor the chocolate pie, sip the chardonnay, make love to your husband, read a good book, teach your daughters how to sew. GO PLAY!

Could it be that my questions about life, faith, and frustrations could be answered in one simple command? Go play? That's exactly what I wanted *my* children to do when they were bored and moaning and groaning about everything in life. I desired more than anything for them to stop complaining and bickering and go play! To enjoy what we had purchased for them! To enjoy the beauty of their lives! Could it possibly be that the God of the universe wanted the same for his child? For me to honor him through my enjoyment of what he's blessed me with?

My perspective shifted, as it usually does when the Almighty has words with me, and a slow smile crept across my face as I poured myself a glass of chardonnay and headed to the back porch to sit with my husband. As I opened the door, still slightly hesitant about leaving numerous tasks undone, I heard a whisper laced with joy, which urged me forward:

Yes, my child, go play.

I was given a church cookbook during my first year of marriage to Jason, with a recipe similar to this one, and I made it often because it was a favorite of his. Since then, I've added and replaced ingredients and have landed upon this version, which is super simple and delicious and still a favorite in my house!

- 2 pounds hamburger
- 1 white onion, diced
- 2 cloves of garlic, diced
- 2 cans cream of mushroom soup
- 8-ounce package of mushrooms, diced
- 8-ounce package of cream cheese
- 2 tbsp Worcestershire sauce
- 2 tsp basil

- 2 tsp oregano
- Salt and pepper to taste
- One package frozen peas

Brown hamburger with onion and garlic. Add remaining ingredients and simmer on low for about 20 minutes. Serve over egg noodles.

8

A WELL-OILED MACHINE

Understanding *How* Your *Family Works*

If you were to peek into our home around 8:00 a.m., a week after Ryan and I returned from our blissful honeymoon in Mexico, you might hear something like, "Caleb! You want a waffle? Chocolate chip, blueberry, or plain? How many? What? I can't hear you! Okay three plain waffles. Syrup? Tate, did you say Pop-Tart? Got it. Hey, Honey! Mabel wants cereal! Can you pour her a bowl? Caleb, another waffle? Okay, just a second. Honey! Can you pop a strudel in for Josh and Jada? Mya wants oatmeal with blueberries? Okay, right, I'll get that in a minute!"

Extreme madness. In my previous life, I had two children (Caleb and Mabel—Lucas was nonverbal and always wanted the same Eggo waffles, and Josh was a newborn) who had opinions about what they ate or didn't eat, and it wasn't a big deal to ask for preferences. Ryan also had two children with opinions, Tate and Mya. In our new family, we had seven children with strong opinions, and within a week of being short-order cooks and feeling like we completed a marathon an hour into every day, we nixed the options. We started slowly—offering this or that—and then simplified even further with one main selection. If cereal was offered, there were two or three options. Oatmeal—topping choices. We've also limited beverage choices to water 90 percent of the time, outside of special occasions. Any possible place we can simplify and teach life skills, we have. I need peace and order, and even with our current reality with eight children, we do manage to achieve this to some extent—but I've had to release control in many other areas.

For example, my house is not perfectly organized and clean by any stretch of the imagination. In my former life, I stressed myself out to tears before a dinner party as I shooed my small children out of the kitchen and scrubbed the tile grout lines for hours—with a toothbrush—*because everyone notices how clean your grout is, right?* I was obsessed with the idea of perfection. Yes, Enneagram 1 raising her hand high here! I have chosen to release this facet of control—I have to with eight children! My house is clean but not perfect, and please don't look in my closets or wipe the windowsills with your finger. Clutter doesn't bother me until it does, and then I feel a desperate need to deep clean my entire house and send half our belongings off to Goodwill. I also detest laundry, and my family has been known to wrap themselves in crunchy towels a time or two.

We've managed to get a grip on what could be constant chaos by incorporating a few reliable, consistent strategies. These systems ensure a semi-loose structure of organized chaos so that we can maintain a semblance of sanity in the middle of the madness, and many of these strategies involve a combination of what worked in our past lives.

Because Ryan's past involved a reality with another woman, he possessed a pattern of accomplishing tasks aligned with a system that he and Kaci felt comfortable with. Jason and I had the same—a pattern of doing life that worked for us. My upbringing as the oldest of twelve also lent to many tried-and-true strategies that I've now incorporated. All families have these systems that are unique and natural, ways of maneuvering that become established with time. When we found ourselves thrust into a new life with seven children—a new life with former systems that worked in those lives—we had to figure out how to make something work in our current life where everyone felt seen, heard, and comfortable. This vision didn't occur overnight, and instead took a year of trial and error, and to this day is a constant, evolving conversation we have as our children age. Here are a few of our favorite organizational systems (but the kids might not agree).

The Bin

The bin is by far the most useful and consistent tool we use, and its presence has been in place from our first year together. I was raised with this system and loathed it with every cell of my being, but I now understand its value. The structure has changed throughout the years to accommodate our kids as they age, but the premise stays the same. First, there is a big, plastic bin. Second, our kids each receive an allowance and, in exchange, are expected to complete daily chores and help clean the house on Saturday morning. Third, if they leave a belonging out at the end of the day: shoes, a game, a favorite toy, a gum wrapper hidden behind a chair, these items are promptly placed in the bin. Every Friday the contents of the bin are divvied up according to each child, and each of these cost a quarter, which is subtracted from their allowance. If a child disobeys or backtalks or lies or steals or hits or whatever, we have a list in place that details the monetary value of these offenses, and a ticket is written and placed in the bin. For example, lying and hitting cost a dollar. Disobedience is a quarter. About once a week, I will offer a list of credits—a mercy list of chores that the kids can take advantage of if they want to redeem some of their tickets or items. Each credit is worth anywhere from a quarter to five dollars—depending on the level of difficulty. It's all tallied up on Friday, and the children are presented with whatever remaining allowance they earned. Those who earn at least half their allowance get to participate in an extra treat, such as an ice cream sundae bar or a box of candy of their choice. The sweets seem to motivate as much as the allowance!

Laundry Bins

As I mentioned earlier, laundry is the bane of my existence. To remedy the never-ending piles and piles and piles of dirty clothes, we purchased a laundry basket for each member of the family and wrote their name on it. There are seven days of the week. Each child (except for Lucas and Annabelle) has a day of the week to do their laundry. *Only that day*. They wash, dry, and put away their clothes. Yes, ten-year-olds are fully capable of working a washing machine; however, they do seem to lack in the folding department. I work my laundry in whenever I can find time, and I also do Lucas's and Annabelle's—however, Annabelle's days are numbered. This system has greatly reduced my stress over dirty clothes everywhere and trying to determine who has clean clothes and who does not.

Chores

Each child has a nightly chore, such as cleaning the table, setting the table, taking the trash out, or sweeping the floor. If they don't do a chore well, or they forget to do it altogether, or they need multiple reminders, they get a ticket—refer back to "The Bin." We also clean the house on Saturday morning. One family member has kitchen duty, another has living room, another has the basement, and so on. By incorporating this method, we manage to clean our entire house in about an hour, and if it's a job well done, there's a reward, which usually involves family time: bowling, a movie night, or shakes at the local ice cream shop. My children are very motivated by ice cream.

Today our life includes an early morning wake-up call at 6:00 a.m., and Ryan is out the door with the kids at 6:30. The kids shower before bed, and we offer easy, quick, mess-free, healthy breakfast options for them to grab, like yogurt, fruit, or Ryan's famous "grab 'em and go" waffles.

- 3 cups of flour
- 2 tbsp maple syrup
- 3 tbsp baking powder
- ¼ tsp salt
- 3 cups almond milk
- 2 tsp vanilla extract
- ⅔ cup melted and cooled coconut oil
- Extras: dark chocolate chips, wheat germ, dried cranberries, walnuts, pecans, chia seeds, flaxseed, or whatever else your heart fancies

Heat the waffle iron. Mix the dry ingredients together and then add the wet ingredients one by one. Mix until well blended and then stir in any extras you want to add. Brush the waffle iron with a little oil or butter to prevent sticking: *This is a major step that you don't want to forget, or you'll have a mess on your hands like I did.* Cook for 5 minutes or so or until the indicator light tells you they're finished.

Prayer Sticks: Faith Practices

As the Thanksgiving table is cleared and December is ushered in, the Christmas cards slowly begin to arrive, bringing glad tidings and good cheer. Many of these creations showcase a beautiful family photo, smiles coming to our little corner of the world from loved ones coast to coast. We rip open the envelopes, eager to admire the images of friends and family who we haven't seen in a while. These cards are hung on an indoor clothesline—a rustic concept that graces the big bay window in our family room (and an attempt at Pinterest creativity from yours truly). I love, love, love Christmas with every ounce of my soul, but—on December 26 at 8:00 a.m., I am over the whole *shebang*. My holiday cheer meter is down to zero. My introverted self is spent. I have no more merry tidings or goodwill toward any men or women. Now granted, I am one of those people who loves to start the holiday magic as soon as the turkey is cleared from the table in late November. True story, we've ventured out in search of the perfect tree on many a Thanksgiving Eve, but after the rush of Christmas Day, I'm cooked as well done as the turkey that graced my table a month prior.

One day post-Christmas, I'm up and at 'em, and as soon as the rich dark coffee beans hit my bones, the evergreen tree which was lovingly picked out only thirty days prior is quickly chucked out the back door and given a firm push of encouragement down the hill. I'm eternally optimistic that this action will be enough to land it resolutely in the river bed, where it will slowly decompose for the next fifty years. Next up is finding a proper home for each of the gifts that were unwrapped from the previous night's festivities, and then last but not least, I gently wrap ceramic baby Jesus and his momma (and the whole crew) back in tissue paper and place them in the plastic bins from whence they came. Finally, the kids arise from their excessive festivities–induced comas, eat the breakfast laid out before them—usually leftover cinnamon rolls from Christmas brunch—and once they have a tiny bit of bounce in their step, I resolutely plop a pile of Christmas cards in front of their weary little faces, along with a couple of safety scissors, and say in the merriest postholiday voice I can muster, "Okay, you know the drill. Start chopping!"

You see, as soon as the holiday ends and the cards are carefully removed from the clothesline, we gather around the kitchen table and promptly chop the heads off photos. These heads will be firmly glued to a popsicle stick, and we will pray for these people throughout the coming year during our devotion time.

Routinely, at 7:30 p.m., the freshly showered crew gathers in the living room, and each family member retrieves a prayer head from a porcelain pot strategically placed on the fireplace mantel—strategically placed high enough so that our youngest can't reach the photos and pretend that they're actual popsicles. As we hold our designated stick head, Dad begins the prayer circle. We begin with thankfulness. Our children have become extremely creative in this department. Sometimes they are thankful they had cookies for dessert, sometimes it's that they get to go to school the next day, some are simply thankful it's Tuesday or Wednesday or whatever day it is, but we begin with a spirit of gratefulness, and then move into prayer for the person on our stick. If we don't know the person, it's vague:

Keep Craig healthy. Help Susan sleep well tonight. Help Bobbie make good friends in school.

If we do have a personal relationship with the person, the prayers are more specific:

Help Betty with her cancer. Please help Tommy, as his parents are getting a divorce. Please help John's foot heal.

It's a simple tradition but one that has worked well. The act of slowing down at seven thirty for reflective family time; airing any questions, concerns, or grievances; or simply procrastinating before heading to bed has been a positive tradition, as we remember those in our life, near and far, and remember to end the day with a thankful spirit.

These traditions remain important, but sometimes maintaining consistency is difficult to achieve, with numerous children participating in sports, jobs, and social activities. I've learned to avoid stressing about keeping a rigid schedule, instead grasping learning moments as they arrive—and they do often in the form of current affairs. Our conversations have become the bedrock of our faith as our children mature; however, as parents we can talk about Jesus until we're blue in the face, talk about being saved, talk about going to church, talk about the tenets of our faith, but if we're not tangibly doing something to help others, then as our Savior laments—we're just a loud, annoying, cringey gong.

As the leaders of our family, Ryan and I incorporate service opportunities for our family members through our nonprofit The Lucas Project, where we prepare and deliver meals for exhausted parents. We write encouraging notes to grandparents. We create spa baskets and care packages for caregivers, to show them that we see the hard and holy work they accomplish, all while our older children help with their brother Lucas. It is extremely important to me as a mom to model a spirit of kindness and then insist that my children also extend this spirit of servitude to the world around them.

TAKEAWAYS

I've had hundreds of people carry me through the most difficult times of my life, including my pregnancy with Lucas and a three-year journey with Jason as he slowly lost his battle with cancer. Here is a limited list of what was helpful during these difficult times, and maybe a couple of the suggestions will be helpful to you as you consider how to involve your family in tangible ways to become the hands and feet of Jesus:

- Gift certificates to order pizza or send pizza their way
- Gift certificates to order Schwan's meals
- A yard cleanup / fix-your-house-problems day (A neighborhood church crew offered this to me—very much appreciated!)
- Lawn mowing or weeding garden beds
- Detailing a vehicle
- House cleaning
- Laundry
- Meals
- Childcare
- Christmas gifts for a family struggling financially
- Grocery delivery
- Transportation to and from appointments
- Clothes shopping for the children
- New shoes for the children
- In-home haircuts (or massage or pedicures)

Four-Ingredient Cookies

These cookies are so easy to make that even Josh and Jada are capable of making these—and they're healthy! I make a big batch and throw them in the freezer. They're a perfect complement for a soup or lasagna that's gifted to a family in need.

- 1 cup peanut butter or almond butter
- 1 egg
- ½ cup maple syrup
- ½–1 cup dark chocolate chips

Mix everything together and bake at 350 degrees for about 12–15 minutes.

Pajamas, Sleep, and Unity: Learning to Pick Your Battles

The Ronne kids are awake at the crack of dawn most days—around 6:00 a.m.—which in my opinion is way too early for anyone to have to get moving. But this is our reality, and we've had to figure out ways to successfully manage these early mornings. Our responsible children meander off to bed early in order to wake up on time without assistance. These children (two of them) are exceptionally organized and lay out their school gear, lunch, and belongings the night before so they won't have to think through these options during the wee hours of the day. All of them shower before bed—"shower" being a very loose term when ten-year-old Joshua is involved. And some of them—much to my dismay when I discovered what was going on—chose to wear their school clothes to bed instead of pajamas.

This began as a sneaky process, which was part of my annoyance. If there's anything that bothers me as a parent, it's sneakiness. This child—and it began with just one child—would shower, put on pajamas, and then proceed to go to bed and change out of pajamas and into the following day's clothing. I discovered this trend one evening while checking on everyone after they should have been asleep. Sure enough, they were asleep—most in their pajamas—but this child was in clothing.

"Honey . . . ," I said to my husband, proceeding to disclose my findings about said child donning their school clothes to sleep in.

"It's gross!" I explained and continued. "They each have about ten pairs of pajamas." This was the truth before our simplification process.

"What's the big deal?" he responded nonchalantly. "I always slept in my clothes."

"Yeah . . . (the sarcasm was about to kick in) but you slept anywhere—under a table, on the couch, on the dashboard of a car

. . . ." I rolled my eyes. "Just because you did it as a child doesn't mean it was right."

"Yes, and just because you slept in pajamas every night, in your bed, at 8:00 p.m. on the dot, doesn't make it right either," he replied in annoyance.

We were both silent as we contemplated what the other has said.

I wondered: *Was it worth the argument that was about to ensue? Maybe just a short argument to prove my point . . .*

"Yes," I continued, "but there are patterns of raising children that do suggest a better outcome than others," my know-it-all, firstborn attitude and google searches blossoming into full effect. "The experts would agree that having a child in bed, at a certain time, with the lights out would be the optimal situation for growth, development, and health," I explained.

"Yes, honey," he agreed, "but the experts don't say anything about pajamas versus clothing." He sighed. "A child can get a good night's sleep in either option, and really, if you think about it, they are using higher-level thinking skills and being responsible in making that decision. They are attempting to gain as much sleep as they can before having to wake up for an early morning, and they are being responsible by making sure that they are dressed and ready to go in the mornings. Don't worry about the gross factor. All kids are gross, whether they wear clothes or pajamas to bed. I didn't even brush my teeth for most of my childhood."

"What?! You didn't brush your teeth? Why not?" This was shocking, as I had been a child who brushed her teeth every morning and evening for eighteen years. That's what I was supposed to do as a human being! I couldn't comprehend why someone wouldn't want to brush their teeth.

"Well," I continued with a knowing smirk, "that didn't work out too well, did it?"

Ryan has a long history of dental decay and cavities, whereas I've never had any dental work or any cavities, and this fact was about to become my sticking point.

He patiently explained, "I'm not saying they shouldn't brush their teeth. I'm saying, pick your battles, and the pajama/clothing battle isn't that big a deal."

I wasn't to the point of full agreement, but over the next few days, my heart and attitude began to soften as one by one my children noticed how the trendsetter had more time to sleep by wearing clothes to bed, and one by one they began replacing their pajamas with the following day's outfit after they had showered.

I began to realize that there are some battles that aren't worth the fight, and that yes, as my husband had suggested, kids are generally gross anyway.

Five years later most of my children—except for Mya, who recognizes the grossness of the matter—wear their clothes to bed.

You're not always going to agree in a blended family, or any family for that matter, especially with yours, mine, and ours, but the best way to create respect and harmony is to present a united front as Mom and Dad and lovingly—if at all possible—discuss the source of disagreement behind closed doors. Many of the battles we fight in our marriage probably fall under a similar category as my issue with the clothing versus pajamas. I was raised one way, and Ryan was raised another way. We both agree that there are nonnegotiables, such as getting enough sleep and brushing your teeth, that make for a healthier child, but something like wearing clothing to bed is not detrimental to a child's well-being. It was simply detrimental to my pride.

Take a good hard look—with a microscope if you're a type-A firstborn like me—at some of the issues you're currently facing in your relationship or family life. Is it a battle worth fighting? Is it worth your peace? Is it worth the strife that it will cause? You may have a teenager who refuses to go to the park, even though you really want to have a family day there. Maybe reevaluate *why* you need it to be a family day. Do you really want an individual participating who doesn't want to be there and will probably only cause strife? Say you have an eight-year-old who wants root beer floats for his birthday instead of the traditional birthday cake that you've always made—that *your* family always had while growing up. Is it really worth the battle? Or maybe your husband wants to go to bed thirty minutes earlier than you do because he's tired, and he'd like you to join him. Is it worth the battle? Do you insist on thirty more minutes of Facebook or take it as an honor that your husband wants you beside him in bed?

Try to take the long view, if possible. Many issues are not worth the effort or the peace that you will sacrifice by pursuing them. Acknowledge when you are beating an issue to death and know when to walk away. Train your brain to recognize what is truly important for the health of your relationships and know when to let it go.

TAKEAWAYS

QUESTIONS TO CONSIDER

- What do you need to reevaluate today?
- What battle has been stealing the peace and joy in your relationship or in your family?
- What is one area that you can agree to loosen up in over the next few weeks? Write it down here, and then pray for discipline and the ability to exhibit restraint and kindness when any issues resurface.

9

SUSTENANCE FOR BODY AND SOUL

The *Importance* of *Gathering* for a Meal

After our move out of rural America in 2018 due to Lucas's growing needs and onto a smaller homestead with only two acres, still in Tennessee but closer to the modern conveniences that Nashville offers (more on this in Chapter Twelve), I noticed a lack of peace in my home, and I sometimes thought, *This mothering gig really isn't my thing anymore.* Four teenagers, one with profound special needs, a preteen, a ten-year-old, a nine-year-old, and a four-year-old who has no lack of confidence. It was a lot. Between health and job issues, which led to emotional issues and arguing and backtalk and snarkiness and bad attitudes, and the older children teaching the younger ones lessons they had no business knowing about, the whole thing was a big honkin' cup that overfloweth—or perhaps it was more like a kitchen sink spilling over. My current situation was causing significant stress. And we—the parents—should have immediately steered the ship back on course; but instead, we bickered and complained as we held on for dear life to the life preserver the kids threw us when they made us walk the plank. A tad bit dramatic, but you get the point.

This sudden change in the family dynamic was attributed to a few circumstances: first, everyone was getting older and hormonal and becoming more opinionated, and second, our move to an urban community offered opportunities for activities, sleepovers, and jobs, and the focus slowly shifted from the family unit (a strong unit we had in rural America, where we relied heavily on one another because it was all we had) to an individualized focus—*You take care of you, and I'll take care of me.* As long as the older crew took ownership of themselves: jobs, food, school, homework, play, we didn't question much of anything. We reasoned it was simply a stressful time in our lives and that "this too shall pass."

Then, a few weeks into the stress and chaos, I turned to Ryan and said, "I really miss family dinners."

With the introduction of new jobs, late nights, playdates with neighborhood kids, everyone fending for themselves, and in turn each individual grabbing a bite to eat here or there, family dinner time had become almost obsolete—a rare exception since our conception in 2011. I pondered this and realized it came down to priorities, as other activities had taken the place of family time. These were good, positive, growth-inducing activities, like sports and friends and lessons, but I yearned to return to my top priority as the matriarch of the whole kit and kaboodle—sitting down together for a meal.

For eight years, we religiously came together at the end of the day and enjoyed a meal—until the move. Gathering around the table was not only a priority in rural Tennessee but also a necessity. We didn't have delivery options, and if we were going to eat, I had to prepare food (or Ryan had to hunt for it). In our previous households, before our blended life together, neither of us participated in family dinners very often. We were raising young children, and for a period of time, we were both knee-deep in a terminal diagnosis of a spouse. Meal preparation wasn't a top priority, nor was sitting down to eat. Food was merely something we occasionally picked at in order to stay alive during a difficult period of life.

When Ryan and I married, we instinctively understood that a mealtime tradition would provide a foundation to our success as a blended family—the art of gathering around a table for a home-cooked meal and offering a blessing for not only the food we were about to eat but also for the Lord's faithfulness in our lives. We knew that the table would provide a basis for community and connectedness in our blended home, and the absence of the table would only leave a void and disconnect.

After this realization, we reincorporated family dinner night. The scene looks a little different than it did in rural America, and we eat later—around six o'clock now because of playtime with the neighborhood kids; however, we've made it a requirement for anyone who is home, and my oh my, what a difference it has made.

Lest I give the wrong impression, let me clarify: Our family dinners are not idyllic times spent in the garden of Eden—no, quite the opposite—but they still provide us with valuable time together. Typically gathering around the table begins with me yelling downstairs or outside or all of the above: "Kids! It's dinnertime!"

And then moaning and groaning ensues because that means screen time or playtime has ended, and then the kids begin stampeding to the table like wild hyenas. I wish I could say they settle down as we begin eating, but they don't. There's a quick prayer offered by whoever is the hungriest or by Annabelle, who simply wants to avoid the inevitable (eating): *God, thank you for this day and bless our food and help us to like it.*

Caleb and Josh lead the pack, eating for efficiency, eating for fuel, and not tasting a single morsel yet not complaining either, so that's a win. The rest suspiciously survey whatever has been placed in front of them. Some immediately decide they won't like it, and pick and moan but eventually get around to eating because there comes a point—and that point occurs when the majority of the family has left the table to begin their chores—when dessert is no longer an option (yes, more on that to come). Usually that point occurs around the thirty-minute marker. Once in a blue moon, when all the stars align, a child will enthusiastically dive into the food and, after testing a small bite, announce the wonder of what they tasted to the rest of us. Those moments make me swoon.

Attitudes have changed and lightened as we laugh around the table, partaking in fresh pasta and warm bread. I love sharing times like these with my children, and I hope they feel the same as the focus shifts and we get to know each other on a heart level, on a real level, rather than simply coexisting under the same roof.

There is so much chatter in the world today about how lonely we are, how depressed and isolated and longing for community we can be, and this is not only true for ourselves as adults; it's also true for our children. Our homes need to be safe places of respect and connections, and what better way to foster these desperately needed essentials than around a table? What better way to encourage conversations? And what better way to show love than to invest our time, our most precious commodity, in our children? Give it a try. You won't regret it.

Zucchini Casserole

This is a recipe I concocted after our move back to a more urban setting. Ryan always grows an overabundance of this vegetable in our (albeit smaller) garden, and I'm forever figuring out ways to incorporate it into our meals. This casserole is a huge hit.

- 2 large zucchinis, diced
- 1 lb breakfast sausage
- ½ cup butter (1 stick)
- ¼ cup nutritional yeast
- 2–3 cups rice (we like black rice)
- 2 cups whipping cream
- Salt and pepper to taste
- ¾ cup Manchego cheese
- ¾ cup parmesan cheese

Cook the rice according to the package directions. (I like to cook my rice with bone broth, which adds more flavor.) Set aside. Sauté the diced zucchini with the sausage. When cooked through, drain off the liquid and set these aside. To make the cream sauce, melt the butter in a large Dutch oven. Slowly add the whipping cream and bring to a boil. Immediately simmer for 5 minutes. Stirring occasionally. Turn the burner off and slowly stir in the cheese, nutritional yeast, and salt and pepper. Turn the burner back on and simmer for 1 minute. Turn off the burner and add sausage, zucchini, and rice to the cheese mixture. Top with more cheese, if desired. Bake at 350 degrees for 20–30 minutes.

Spinach: The Importance of Maintaining Our Health

While Ryan and I were dating, we never had a conversation about how food preferences would play a role in our relationship, and honestly, we were so love struck during our quick courting period that we couldn't eat more than a slice of pizza when we were together. I knew he enjoyed foods and drinks that had never been in my home before (Mountain Dew, Hamburger Helper, and Pop-Tarts) and that I had a strong aversion to because of their lack of nutrition. I was a fresh greens, water, organic meat, organic fruit, organic everything type of gal, and that's how I was raising my children, so help me God. I snuck a bag of spinach into anything and everything: lasagna, soups, brownies, you name it. My biological kids grew up this way and didn't question the spattering of green in everything they ate. It was an everyday part of life, just like the big bowl of apples offered daily on our kitchen table. One of my proudest mom moments was bringing two-year-old Joshua to Subway and him choosing, unassisted, a ham, cheese, and spinach sandwich.

Jason was also extremely health conscious, and he taught our children the value of healthy choices. He was a tennis professional and personal trainer and could usually be found snacking on raw broccoli and chicken breast. He agreed with my desire to provide clean, healthy, homemade food for the family and oftentimes requested that I step it up a notch!

Ryan, on the other hand, had been living off the kindness of his friends and family for months as they delivered meals which his children often ate; however, he gravitated toward a diet of take-out, soda, and peanut M&Ms. His idea of a vegetable was corn in a can. I have no recollection of why we didn't discuss any of this before marriage, but we didn't. I assumed that as the wife and mother of the house, meal preparation would be my responsibility—as it always had been and because I enjoyed cooking. I didn't think my new husband would buck the system—my system.

Ryan's Take

Changing isn't easy for anyone. I remember those first few weeks after we were married, and they were extremely chaotic. We were trying so hard to help the kids transition into this new life, but they pretty much did whatever they wanted. I am not organized, nor do I come from a large family, and in fact, I'm not very disciplined, so Jess had an uphill battle ahead. She started making lists of chores and cracking down on bedtimes and what healthy foods we were going to add to our diets. I was happy to help support her—until I had to follow the rules! I wasn't used to going to bed early, eating healthy foods, and not having my fridge stocked with Mountain Dew and ice cream. Imagine my shock! She inherited four kids instead of three because I was a horrible influence. I had some terrible habits, and to her credit, she convinced me that she wanted to grow old and gray with me, which meant I had to change a couple of bad habits. It wasn't easy and I hate to admit it, but I'm glad she encouraged me to change. I rarely drink any form of pop, I have limited my sugar intake drastically, and I have learned to really love vegetables. That's right, Mom, I *love* vegetables. I love them so much I create a huge garden of veggies every summer. Full of tomatoes, peppers, green beans, squash, zucchini—you get the picture. We try our best to can what we don't eat and often eat from the garden until the next one is planted. I have noticed that the more I enjoy healthier foods, the more our kids are willing to at least try to like them.

Mealtime as a family was important as we entered our marriage because while we spent months on end caring for our sick spouses, we often ate meals on the go, in between caring for our children and fulfilling the duties of our marriages, in sickness and in health. We were eager to return to a routine.

I remember the first "aha" moment I had as the new wife and mom of our blended household. We gathered around our big dining room table, and I presented homemade bread (from the bread maker) and lasagna with chopped-up spinach spattered throughout the sauce. This was a typical lasagna for my biological children, and they ate with gusto. Ryan and his children scrunched up their faces in disgust as they peered at what was before them and then proceeded to pick each tiny speck of green out of the lasagna (the kids, not Ryan). At the time, our relationship was too new for me to insist that they eat the spinach, and I let it go, knowing that I would address the issue that evening with their father.

Ryan later explained: "Tate and Mya have probably never had spinach, let alone spinach scattered throughout a favorite dish of theirs—lasagna."

I listened.

He agreed that the green addition was a beneficial way to gain lots of healthy nutrients for both the kids and himself, and then suggested, "Perhaps you could use the food processor to chop it up so that it doesn't appear so slimy and noticeable?"

I halfheartedly agreed to try this tactic and, surprisingly, it worked. All these years later, a bag of spinach still finds its way into many of my dishes, and I don't have to chop it up anymore because now its presence is normal to everyone.

But, believe me, we've had that pokey, stubborn child who upon looking at whatever is offered, outside of hotdogs and hamburgers, immediately decides that he or she is going to become the slowest eater ever. I believe many of us are familiar with this child.

I can hear the questions: *But what if they truly don't like something?* Or, *What if they starve?*

Our children don't have to eat anything they don't like; however, we do have a couple of incentives in place to curb extreme pickiness.

Each child can pick one food they absolutely detest, and they don't have to eat this food ever. Some of the options in the past have included sauerkraut, oatmeal, grits, and collard greens. Mine has always been eggs. I detest eggs. Also, we offer dessert every night, and this addition seems to be a very effective motivator. If I'm serving a unique dinner that might be viewed suspiciously, dessert becomes a triple-decker homemade chocolate cake with ice cream. You'd be amazed at how quickly a child will eat with this in front of their face. Other times, it's fresh fruit, but the consistent rule is this: the only way to get dessert is to eat what's on your plate. Finally, we don't snack often. I've read a few books on how French children will eat almost anything, and we have incorporated many French principles into our household, including minimal snacking. We have unlimited breakfast, lunch, and dinner. In other words, eat until you're full—and there is always plenty! If we eat dinner later than usual, I might offer fresh veggies with ranch or a cut-up watermelon or hummus with pretzels, but generally, we eat at mealtime and eating will occur because we're hungry.

My goal as a mom is to one day release my offspring into the wide, grand, exciting world of food and have them be familiar, on some level, with most of what they encounter because I introduced it to them once upon a time. We've tried crab cakes and cashew cheese and sauerkraut and spaghetti squash and kombucha and venison and fried crickets and street tacos and brisket and jalapeno poppers and beet soup and liver pate and collard greens, to name a few. I believe the key to encouraging our children to eat this wide assortment of foods can be attributed to a few principles.

1. Honest conversations about how our food choices either harm or heal our bodies. (My kids understand this—even if they don't always like it.)
2. Mom and Dad eat everything that the kids eat (sometimes Dad becomes really subdued as he slowly forks the food into his mouth, but he eats it!), and we try to make it fun with a reward in place, like dessert.
3. I believe in the importance of children understanding where their food comes from, which was the driving force behind our move to rural Tennessee. During our time on our homestead, our kids helped tend the garden, they had a say in what we grew, and they saw the miracle

unfold before their eyes when the tomatoes ripened and the beans were ready to be picked. They helped Mom make jam and can fresh produce. They raised chickens and defeathered them after they were butchered. They knew that the venison in our freezer came from our backyard, and that the turkey we ate was raised by the farmer down the road. They knew where their eggs came from and how bread is made with flour, yeast, and water. Because of this experience, they have a deep abiding understanding of where their food comes from, and this is important for children to learn.

Lasagna with Spinach

Here's a family favorite and a meal that's become commonplace in our home and around our table.

- 1 pound sausage
- 1 pound hamburger
- 8–10 portabella mushrooms, diced (optional)
- 1 onion, diced
- 5 garlic cloves, diced
- Olive oil
- 2 14-ounce cans diced tomatoes
- 2 6-ounce cans tomato paste
- Salt and pepper to taste
- Basil and oregano to taste
- A bag of fresh spinach
- 2 eggs
- ½ cup parmesan cheese or nutritional yeast
- 2 cups cottage cheese
- 1–2 cups Mozzarella cheese
- 10 lasagna noodles

Cook the noodles according to the package directions, adding a tablespoon of olive oil to avoid sticking. Set aside. Sauté the onion, garlic, sausage, and hamburger together and drain. Return the mixture to the pan and add the tomatoes, tomato paste, spinach, salt, pepper, basil, and oregano. Simmer for 30 minutes. In the meantime, combine the eggs, cottage cheese, and either parmesan cheese or nutritional yeast in a bowl.

Next up is assembly! Lay four noodles down flat in a 9×13 pan. Add half of the cottage cheese mixture. Add half of the meat mixture next, and add some cheese or nutritional yeast on top of that. Repeat the layers again, and top with mozzarella cheese or yeast. Cover with foil and bake at 350 degrees for 30 minutes. Remove the foil and continue baking for an additional 10 minutes.

Ryan swears this lasagna only gets better with time and often begs me to make two pans of it so he can enjoy it for lunch throughout the week.

Cheap Eats: Feeding the Family on a Budget

Feeding a large crew can quickly become an expensive undertaking—especially with a focus on health because anything organic or non-GMO or minimally processed is going to cost more than junk food (but that's a whole other book). I do everything in my power to make our grocery budget go as far as it possibly can. We've always raised chickens for meat and eggs. We preserve sauces, salsas, relishes, peppers, and tomatoes from our garden. I browse the clearance racks at the grocery store. I use coupons, and I shop in season. However, the number-one way I save money on groceries is by making most of our meals from scratch.

Cooking is an outlet as I relax and unwind after a busy day. I often have the kids help with the preparations in the morning, slicing or dicing the fruit or vegetables or making a side dish to accompany the meal, like homemade yeast rolls—which Mya can make in her sleep at this point—or applesauce, which is as easy as cutting a bunch of apples (skins left on), putting them in a pot filled with water, sprinkling cinnamon on top, and simmering on low all day. This is a super easy and healthy addition to many of our meals, and the wafting smell of apples and cinnamon makes our house smell heavenly. I also love using dry beans and rice—which are an incredibly satisfying and inexpensive way to fill bellies. Soups are a healthy, economical way to incorporate these fillers. Beans and rice are easily purchased in bulk, and if stored in a cool, dark place—or even the freezer—will last forever.

It's not cheap to feed a family of ten, but I have unearthed a few tricks through the years. In many diverse cultures, pasta, grains, and beans are used in much greater quantities, and meat is limited. These are great filler options and much less expensive than chicken or beef. My family doesn't respond positively to zero meat (vegetarian week was not popular), but they don't notice if I reduce the quantity. As long as they get that occasional bite of sausage or chicken, they are happy and don't feel deprived, and of course, there's always plenty of food and the enticement of dessert. Not only have we been able to feed our large crew on a budget, but we're all healthier as well. Here are two versions of chicken soup that I often make in the cooler winter months. I'll cook a whole chicken or maybe two of them overnight on low and then use the meat to make (and freeze) the following two soups, which go great with Mya's rolls. I also use the carcass to make gallons of bone broth—which will also freeze. But before we dive into the soup recipes, here are a few primers on chicken, beans, soup base, and broth.

Chicken Prep

Preheat the oven to 200 degrees right before bed (for us, around 10:00 p.m.). Place the chicken in a Dutch oven or a big cooking pot. Cut a lemon in half and squeeze the juice all over the skin of the bird. Season with salt, pepper, and thyme (or whatever else you like). Bake covered overnight. Remove first thing in the morning and let cool before enlisting the help of one of your children or your hubby to remove the chicken from the bones. My kids are not a fan of this chore. Honestly, it's not my favorite either.

How to Cook Dry Beans: Way Cheaper Than Canned

Confession time—I never sort the beans. Who cares if one is broken? Doesn't matter to me one bit. In the morning, I'll add a few cups of beans—about three cups for our family—and then fill a pot up with water or bone broth. Bring this to a boil, cover, and simmer all day. Every hour or so, test to see if the beans are soft. If not, keep simmering. You might have to add water throughout the process or do an overnight soak, which is explained on the bag. I usually forget about beans until the day I need them, so this often isn't an option for me.

Soup Base

Sauté an onion and a few garlic cloves in some olive oil, butter, ghee, or a combination of the three. Sauté until the onion is transparent. Remember to stir so that you don't burn the garlic!

Homemade Bone Broth

Take the chicken carcass and bones and place them in a Crock-Pot. Fill to the top with filtered water and add 1/2 cup of apple cider vinegar (which draws out the nutrients). Add spices, leftover vegetables, and whatever you want to the pot—I don't get too crazy here. Cook on low for 24 hours. Let cool and then pour into glass jars. Redo the process two or three more times until the bones become brittle and then throw them away. This will last in the fridge for about a week or for months in the freezer.

The following are two soup options using one whole chicken. Make the soup base and then follow the directions for each.

Chicken Noodle

- Soup base
- ½ of the chicken cut into small pieces
- 2 cups carrots, diced
- 2 cups celery, diced
- 1 16-ounce package of egg noodles (cooked according to package directions)
- Bone broth
- 1 tsp thyme
- Salt and pepper to taste

After the onions are transparent in the soup base, add the carrots and celery and cook for a few minutes, stirring occasionally. Add the remaining ingredients, except for the noodles and chicken. Simmer on low for 30 minutes. Add the noodles and boil right in the soup according to the bag. Turn the stove off and add the chicken. Enjoy!

Chicken Chili

- Chicken cut into pieces (½ of the chicken you cooked overnight)
- 48 ounces of cooked and drained great northern beans
- Soup base
- 1 jar (16 oz) of your favorite salsa
- 2 tsp cumin
- Salt and pepper to taste
- Broth to fill the pot
- 1 8-ounce package of shredded Monterey Jack cheese

Mix all the ingredients together in a pot. Simmer 1 hour, stirring occasionally. Top with additional cheese, if desired.

Mya's Easy Homemade Rolls

- 2 cups warm water
- ½ cup sugar
- 1½ tbsp active dry yeast
- 1½ tsp salt
- ¼ cup olive oil
- 5–6 cups bread flour

In a large bowl, dissolve the sugar in warm water. Add the yeast and let proof for 5 minutes. Add the salt and oil, and then slowly add the flour. Mix well and then knead for 10 minutes. Place in a well-oiled bowl and cover with a damp towel. Allow to rise until doubled in size—about an hour. Punch the dough down and divide into small balls—about 12–15. Place the dough balls on a well-greased cookie sheet and allow to rise for about 30 minutes. Bake at 350 degrees for 20 minutes.

10

PURSUING FAMILY TIME AND REST

Making *Room* for What's Truly *Important*

Pick an object, any object, and we probably had 500 billion of said object as soon as the boxes from our two households were unpacked. Shoes? Yep. Toothbrushes. Pencils—I counted out of curiosity and reached five hundred before dropping the pursuit and instead found an empty box and marked it *Donations*. Towels. Wet towels. Ridiculous squishy stress-reliever creatures, bags of flour, bathing suits, bikes, erasers, markers, crayons, toys, liners for Lucas's diapers, sheets, hammers, screwdrivers, video games, DVDs, mops, brooms, and on and on and on. At one point, I counted twenty-eight pairs of blue jeans in one daughter's closet. Twenty-eight pairs. This outrageousness was evident everywhere.

The sheer number of belongings was not only exhausting, but it hampered my desire to pursue a more minimalist lifestyle. And magically, somehow, as soon as I drove off to Goodwill with a few boxes, more treasures seemed to pop up overnight. As if the

Almighty was raining down goodies as my children slept! It gives me anxiety.

This excess and overabundance arrived hand in hand with our commingling as a family, when our belongings were immediately doubled or quadrupled. With our blended union, our children now had twenty-two grandparents—yep, a recipe for extravagance if there ever was one. Excessiveness with three children isn't such a big problem; however, excessiveness with eight becomes a problem very quickly.

When Ryan, Tate, Mya, and Jada moved to Michigan, we unloaded approximately thirty big plastic bins full of random stuff into our dining room, and these bins filled the entire room, leaving it unusable for the first few months. These were in addition to everything I also contributed.

In those early, blissful days, I awoke bright and early, eager to tackle the chaos after the children skedaddled off to school. I'd make myself comfortable, lift a lid, and stare at the contents. Two hundred rolls of toilet paper. Hundreds of unopened note cards. Pens, notepads, and unused picture frames. I began what I believed to be the natural process of purging, and as I would place an item in a box marked for Goodwill, Ryan would curiously (annoyingly) ask, "You don't think we'll use that?" because in his logical thought process, there might be a slight possibility that the whole world might someday run out of this particular item—this was prior to the 2020 worldwide pandemic when he could have had a major *I told you so* attitude with the toilet paper.

I didn't live this way before Ryan and purged often and quickly. Jason and I desperately needed money as he struggled to work during his cancer treatments, and I sold any unnecessary items we owned. Also, excessiveness is stressful for me. I function better when my outward life is organized and free from clutter, as I believe most of us do. Ryan and I had our work cut out for us, and first on the agenda was seeking to understand why we each brought different thought patterns to the relationship when it came to belongings.

Ryan didn't have much growing up and was often envious of what others possessed. He grew up with a single mom who worked hard to provide for the family. Each new school year, she purchased two pairs of blue jeans (often used), a few shirts, and a pair of shoes, and these were expected to last him throughout the year. Ryan pitied his mom and tried to lighten her load by making his own money.

My background was different. My parents imposed strict rules about taking care of our belongings, but we didn't want for anything. My dad was an attorney and my mom was a mom. We received a limited wardrobe at the beginning of the school year—always consisting of brand-new clothes—and if we outgrew them, we were given more new clothes. Our daily necessities were provided, unless we wanted a particular brand instead of what was purchased. We earned an allowance in exchange for our chores, witnessed Mom and Dad go on date nights, occasionally went out to eat as a family, vacationed in our travel trailer, and were secure in the knowledge that our parents had enough money to take care of us.

The process of understanding our differences has been slow. Ryan eventually understood how the clutter was going to control our lives if we didn't get control over it, and how my mental health was more important than all that stuff. We eventually arrived at a compromise. I could donate items, but he wanted to remain ignorant about what was donated to avoid feeling guilty—as if we were throwing away money. Fair enough. I had no problem decluttering without him.

Managing belongings and then decluttering takes time, and time is the one commodity that is continuously lost. Aging has brought us clarity about how we want to spend our time—with each other and our loved ones, not on maintaining our excessive belongings.

Most everyone, I think, functions optimally with a semblance of order. I read once that an organized home makes a productive home, and while I wouldn't call us completely organized, we do seek to bring order to our busy lives through small steps.

We've incorporated the following solutions in our quest to become a more organized, well-oiled Ronne machine. I would encourage anyone who feels overwhelmed by clutter to implement one or two of these solutions, and maybe you'll find a few pockets of time for yourself as your children learn responsibility and independence.

TAKEAWAYS

- *The towel issue, or more specifically, "Who left this wet towel on the floor?!"* One Christmas, I suggested to the crafty grandma the idea of embroidering the name of each child on a specific colored towel, and that would be their towel. Period. We eliminated the rest of the towels—except for the nice ones in the master bathroom. This system has worked beautifully. No longer do I wonder whose wet towel is on the floor. I know exactly whose it is, and if it remains there until the end of the day, it's headed to the bin.
- *Socks.* Another headache was trying to determine who took their stinky socks off midday and left them lying in the middle of the floor or by the trampoline or in the van. Now each child has seven pairs of a specific type of sock. For example, Annabelle's all have lace trim, Mabel's

are plain colors, Mya's are patterns, and Jada has white or gray. The boys have their specifics as well. If they wear out a pair of socks, they are welcomed (and encouraged) to turn in the worn-out pair, and I will then give them a new pair. If they have simply lost their socks, they are welcomed to purchase a new pair for a quarter. Responsibility lessons at play here.

- *Toiletries.* The same rule applies here as it does for the socks. Each child has a bath caddy—a cheap plastic caddy from the dollar store. In this caddy, they store their towel, shampoo, conditioner, toothbrush, hairbrush, deodorant, toothpaste, and whatever else they need. When they bring me the empty tube of that product, I give them a replacement.
- *Presents.* We've suggested to the grandparents that in lieu of gifts for holidays and birthdays, we would appreciate money so that we can spend time together making memories. Most have enthusiastically embraced this suggestion.

My Favorite Cocktail

Some of my favorite purge sessions have involved late nights with Ryan as we sorted through items, me throwing them in the Goodwill box, him extolling the redeeming qualities of a particular item, and me swallowing down what I want to say with a sip of my spritzer. Here you have it—a spritzer that's refreshing for those stressful moments. Feel free to eliminate the wine for a healthy mocktail version.

- 1 tsp of elderberry syrup
- Pineapple LaCroix sparkling water
- A splash of chardonnay

Campfires: Incorporating Relaxing Traditions

Fall in Tennessee can be a bit unpredictable. Many days are blazing hot—100 degrees, with humidity thick like molasses. Other days are cool and brisk and have us bundling up in sweaters and blankets to warm our chilled bones; however, overall, fall in Tennessee is absolutely perfect. The warmth of a 70-degree day, sun high in the sky, chilled, gentle air sweeping away any perspiration that may transpire, and perfect for outdoor activities like walking, gardening, biking, or fishing, to name a few. The evenings bring a cool bite as the days shorten and the nights become longer, and the sky is so clear you can count a million stars—if you didn't have a million kids and had the time.

Family fun takes priority on nights like these—priority over healthy meals and nutritional options—and this doesn't occur often in our household. I purchase seventy-seven-cent packages of hotdogs; white, enriched, cheap Walmart buns; Hershey's chocolate; graham crackers; and marshmallows. I might add a salad or side that contributes a bit of nutrition if I'm feeling ambitious, and a big tub of "just add water" lemonade. The crew rumbles with excitement as the older ones gather firewood and the little ones search for kindling. Inevitably, there's a child or two who becomes sidetracked, and instead of gathering wood for the fire, he or she begins to search for roasting sticks and chairs for Mom and Dad. They're beyond eager and ready to burst smack dab into the fun festivities, but rest assured, their older siblings will steer them back on track with a friendly, reminder: "Hey! We don't need chairs or roasting sticks yet! We're supposed to gather wood! Don't you know anything?!"

Our firepit is a big open hole that Ryan dug and constructed out of huge rocks he found on our property, and in place of traditional chairs, we have logs around the perimeter for the kids. Ryan and I are too old to sit on uncomfortable logs, so we call the two bright-red padded chairs for our weary behinds.

Once we're comfortably settled, we say a quick prayer and then split open the hotdog package as the vultures dive in. Dog after dog after dog—two or three packages ripped into and devoured. The kids love it because there is no limit to their ridiculous, ravenous appetites when we do a campfire. Even Lucas enjoys these occasions—when the air is cool and the food is flowing. He is an eager participant for any occasion when the sustenance is plentiful! Aren't we all? He becomes mesmerized by the hot, red flames, dancing into the night sky, as he devours his fill—dog after dog after dog. We pacify him with food until he begins throwing it on the ground and the chickens race to see who can retrieve the precious commodity first. Lucas smiles as the commotion awakens his senses.

The other kids can party all night, eating, enjoying family time, chasing fireflies, and while the flames dance against the dark backdrop of the night sky, Ryan and I settle in—Ryan with his processed dog and me with my veggie option. We slowly sip on ice-cold beverages and enjoy the slower pace this sacred time gifts us as a family—little bodies dancing, throwing sticks into the fire, getting a little too close to the flames until one of us hollers, "Stop playing with the fire! You're going to get burned!"

And eventually, as the hours tick on by, our numbers begin to dwindle, and Dad heads indoors with Lucas as his demands get louder: "All done! All done! Take a bath! Take a bath!" He's confused about the change in his normal routine: bath, pajamas, movie, and lights out. The kids are finally full and begin working off their gluttony with bike riding or basketball, while I clean up the mess, putting leftovers in Ziploc bags (if there are any) and scooping salad remains into plastic containers.

These are truly the happiest (and least expensive!) times we spend together as a family. These are the moments that make a life—that make a family—moments of slowing down, taking a breather, being present, engaging in life, putting away the cell phones, and embracing the beauty of nature. This gift can occur in rural Tennessee under the night sky, or it can be experienced on a rooftop in New York City. It is a state of mind rather than a location.

We are often so caught up in the day-to-day grind and what's next that we forget to stop. We forget to be present. We forget to dump the rules (or the seventy-seven-cent packages which held our dinner), and if we forget enough times, we will wake up one day and find that we forget right into nothingness. There will be no memories with our families. There will be no happy fire dances. There will be nothing but paychecks and calls with clients and strained relationships with kids and spouses and then death. Mae West said, "We only live once, but if we do it right, once is enough."

Schedule a campfire today. Or a day at the park. Or perhaps bowling. Whatever family time looks like for your family, put it on the calendar and then prioritize it—at least once a month. These are the moments that make a life.

Potato Salad

I usually make this potato salad the day before our campfire. It's really simple and inexpensive, and the flavors develop over time in the fridge.

- 10–12 large potatoes, scrubbed clean and boiled until soft
- Mayo to taste
- 2 tbsp mustard
- One 8-ounce jar of sweet pickle relish
- 1–2 tsp paprika
- Salt and pepper to taste

- 1 heaping tbsp or more of dill
- A dash of cayenne (if you like a little kick)
- 1 onion, diced

Let the potatoes cool and then dice them and put them in a bowl. Add the rest of the ingredients and stir well. Refrigerate until cool.

Sabbath: Making Time for Rest in Order to Recharge

Ryan and I are busy people. We thrive on productivity and struggle to stop working. Part of this "get 'er done" spirit is related to the PTSD we often experience as caregivers to Lucas. It's difficult to explain how PTSD is related to caregiving, and admittedly, it's not to the extreme of that experienced by a soldier after combat. I'm not going to literally die at any minute, but it's present nonetheless. The idea of rest is elusive because if I let my guard down and actually take a moment, close my eyes, or watch a cooking show on Netflix, more often than not, I will almost immediately hear an inevitable scream from Lucas, indicating that he is unhappy about something. Or I smell yet another reminder that he needs a new diaper. It's easier to keep my head down and work than to entertain the concept of rest and then suffer disappointment if it doesn't occur or is immediately interrupted.

It is a challenging endeavor to truly find relaxation as caregivers to eight children, and in order to embrace the idea of rest, Ryan and I often leave our home. We do this weekly through date nights together, but we also pursue rest individually.

I grew up in a strict "work then play" household. Yes, that's a sweet little jingle my mother used to say. We worked hard and completed our chores, and then we were rewarded with play. During the summer months, this philosophy involved working in the garden during the cooler morning hours: pulling weeds, watering plants, and picking the produce. After a job well done and the breakfast remains cleared away, we were rewarded with a trip to our grandma's cottage at the lake. This is also how I run my ship—er, home. I appreciate the values that the concept instilled in my life, and I hope to pass along similar values to my offspring.

I struggle with the concept of letting go of productivity, letting go of busyness—really, letting go of control. There is always something I could accomplish: clothes to lay out, papers to sign, backpacks to fill, words to be written, weeds to be pulled, calls to be made, and on and on. I not only struggle with the art of relaxation, but I become envious when my husband doesn't struggle with the concept!

Sundays have a sneaky way of causing an immense amount of anxiety, and I don't believe these are the feelings the Lord intended when he created this day of rest. Everyone in my family understands Sabbath rest except for me. It has to be my martyr mentality—a resentful reasoning that the family wouldn't be able to rest if I wasn't whipping around, making food, getting children dressed for church, tying bows into hairstyles, cleaning dishes, throwing in a few loads of laundry, laying out school clothes for Monday, investigating backpacks to make sure homework is completed, preparing breakfast for Monday, feeding and changing Lucas, bathing the little ones, picking up around the house (so we can wake up to a clean house bright and early Monday morning), and making meal plans and grocery lists for the week. I don't think the list ever ends, so I'll just stop here.

Historically, I'd be busy, busy, busy, and Ryan would say, "I'm going fishing for a few hours while Annabelle sleeps. Okay?"

Not really a question, and I would huff and puff—to make sure he knew I wasn't thrilled about him relaxing, given the tasks that still needed to be completed.

Sometimes he would even prepare me days in advance that he was going fishing because, get this excuse, he needed it! I understood the need, but I didn't understand the freedom, as *Work then play, work then play* would jingle about in my head. *You can't play then work, or even play an entire day when there's work to be done, can you?* I wasn't sure how that would work at all!

There is something noble about the martyr mentality, this desire to be needed as a Godly woman ("She selects wool and flax and works with eager hands" [Prov. 31:13]—every Christian woman's guilt-driven model of holiness) that trumps our Lord's call to be obedient. Yes, we are called to be good mothers, good wives, good housekeepers, but we are also called to honor the Sabbath day and keep it holy (Exod. 20:8).

Nine of the Ronnes have a great understanding of the Sabbath, this having been modeled exceptionally well by their father. However, the other parent in this authoritative equation has not exactly grasped how to fall into the grace of what the Sabbath is meant to be—a day of idyllic reprieve. Moms—raising my hand high here!—love the idea that our families could never survive if we weren't running around like beheaded chickens seven days a week. It's a double-edged sword. We love to be needed, but we resent the work at the same time.

I had to surrender. Wave the white flag. I had to surrender to a higher calling that trumps the unrealistic concept of the Proverbs 31 woman who never lets her candle burn out. I had to surrender to the need to feel fulfilled through my family's desires. I had to surrender to the biblical calling of a Sabbath. I, the mother of many beautiful children and the wife to a wonderful husband, had to choose rest. I was going to read, crochet, write, and watch the Food Network channel. I was going to take my rightful place on the couch and bask in the delightfulness of a much-needed nap. Yes, this was a choice I had to make because there were always activities and chores that needed to be accomplished, but I had to choose a higher calling—an obedience to my Abba Father and his command to rest.

Now when Ryan yells out, "Honey, I'm going fishing for a few hours!" I no longer huff and puff about. Nope. Instead, I smile because I realize that I was given the gift of an entirely peaceful afternoon all to myself (at least until Annabelle wakes up from her nap).

And, bonus, sometimes he brings home the bacon (the fish!) and we feast on fish tacos.

TAKEAWAYS

In our house, we've gotten into a routine where the entire family works hard on Saturdays—cleaning the house or the garage, catching up on laundry, making food for Sunday, or cleaning up the yard. We work diligently on Saturday and then we all relax on Sunday.

I do not cook on Sunday. Breakfast is something easy, like cereal. Lunch consists of make-your-own sandwiches, chips, and fruit. Dinner is also something easy—a cook-out, something on the grill, or frozen pizza. Ryan and I take turns checking on Lucas. If his shift happens to fall on the most incredible touchdown of the year, I will graciously take his turn in exchange for a much-needed foot rub during half-time.

The kids also relax. This means quiet time. Their afternoons are spent playing outside or quietly doing something inside, like reading, writing, scrolling. *Quietly* . . .

I do what brings relaxation and bliss to my soul, and for me this involves the Food Network, a walk, a little yoga, or some light reading.

But of course, relaxation is different for everyone and only you can answer what this looks like in your life. Maybe it's similar to mine, walking or reading, or maybe it's more active like kicking the soccer ball around with your kids or taking a Sunday drive with a friend. Whatever it is, allow yourself this day of rest, which was not commanded out of a religious obligation meant to make us feel guilty but instead is a suggestion born out of our Savior's immense love for us because self-care is soul care.

11

HOLIDAYS, BIRTHDAYS, AND THE TOOTH FAIRY

Blending Traditions and *Creating* New Ones

"Mom! I lost my first tooth!" seven-year-old Joshua exclaimed and then eagerly asked, "Can you get me a dollar?"

The poor kid had been anticipating this moment for so long, losing his first tooth, his mother's genetics to blame. I didn't begin teething until I was nearly two years old, and my biological children followed suit, which led to losing teeth at a much later age than most of their peers. Even more depressing was Joshua's complete disbelief in the tooth fairy at such a young age. His six siblings had lost numerous teeth and, in the process, had lost their belief in the tooth fairy. Because the older siblings no longer believed in this mythical creature, they made sure that their younger siblings knew how foolish that belief was as well. It wasn't only the tooth fairy who got the boot; the Easter bunny, Superman, Elmo, and even Santa Claus were not exempt from the cynical older Ronne children's truth-telling serum. Such is life at the bottom of the barrel in a big family.

A few years into our marriage, our imaginative, unrealistic ideas of utopia also crashed as the rose-colored blinders began to fall off and Ryan and I recognized the difficult reality of our new blended life. Our marriage absolutely resembled a fairy tale in the early stages of bliss. (Don't most relationships?) It was easy to believe that Ryan was perfect and I had fallen in love with my other half. I'm sure he also believed the same about me! I was as beautiful as a princess, and he was as strong as Superman, and I was as sweet as Elmo and he was as giving as Santa Claus. And then time marched on, and the endorphins wore off, and we matured and began to face the undesired but factual truth that we were living in neither Candyland nor Neverland nor anything resembling utopia—unfortunately. We were in the real world, with real people, who had real flaws and resembled characters like the Hulk and Oscar the Grouch and at times Ursula the evil sea witch much more consistently than the beautiful mythical creatures we thought we had fallen in love with.

Why does this happen? Why can't we stay in Candyland? Statistically, the endorphins that allow us to see past our partner's flaws can be maintained, at the absolute most, for approximately two years after marriage. Ryan and I definitely maxed those babies out to the very end of their time limit. We truly were madly, deeply, and googly eyed in love right up until that two-year marker, and then there was a noticeable shift. The reality of who I had married began to surface. In fact, it seemed like he changed overnight when, in fact, he didn't change. I changed when I finally accepted the full spectrum of who he was—flaws and all. I married a man who had scars and battle wounds. Scars from his childhood and wounds from his life prior to me.

His passivity about certain areas of life concerned me—like the junk he left in the yard. I envisioned a garden of Eden, a beautiful yard surrounded by vintage rose bushes and ivy spilling onto the patio and a babbling fountain that soothed our souls, but my vision of utopia was jolted when I looked outside and saw in place of the roses and babbling fountain a bunch of junk everywhere. *Who lived like this and was okay with an old washing machine in their front yard?* I wondered. *Or a bunch of scrap metal littered around the barn? Or flower beds overrun with weeds?* My expectation was that the woman took care of the household and the man took care of the yard work. That's how it had worked in my past. Another big issue was Ryan's desire to keep all the junk. He could not pass on anything that was offered for free, and not only did he never pass on anything; he oftentimes went in search of it! Case in point, he offered to help an older couple move, and they promised him a barn full of treasures in return. Or, speaking of barns, he once offered to tear down an old barn for a friend in exchange for the belongings in the barn, and inevitably, those treasures had to go somewhere. Most landed in our garage, our barns, or our yard—which is how an old washing machine now graced my front yard where the babbling fountain was supposed to go. I should have understood this tendency about my husband from the first time I went to his house, but the endorphins clouded my vision back then.

I arrived in Oklahoma to help him pack for his move to Michigan, and I saw, with my own two eyes, the boxes piled floor to ceiling. When I opened the closet doors, I saw the contents fall to the ground because they were so numerous. I saw the backyard shed overflowing with backup tools, backups to backups of every tool you could imagine, just in case one of them went missing. I witnessed the reality back in those good ole days, but I failed to really understand how these traits might affect me in the future.

In those early days, I blissfully saw my prince charming, but when reality kicked in, he looked more like Shrek—and that's when Ursula the sea witch emerged.

It's amazing how God allows us to perceive a new partner through the eyes of grace for a period of time—a period to really solidify the relationship. However, what's the solution when the grace is lifted and we see this person for who he or she really is—a flawed individual with faults and quirks and irritable personality tendencies? How do we cope with this newly discovered reality?

Acceptance. We accept this person for who they are—flaws and all. The best gift we can give our spouse is unconditional love, which is easier said than done. It's easy to love someone when they are exactly as you want them to be, your distorted vision of perfection, but it's much more difficult when they have a mind of their own. I compare it to an infant versus a teenager. I bet most parents would adamantly agree that it's easier to love a sweet, innocent infant when they are totally dependent on you for their well-being and growth. An infant who gazes into your eyes with adoration and complete dependence. An infant who coos as you introduce her to the art of language. An infant who smiles when you walk into the room. Now contrast this ideal with the infant who grows up and becomes a mouthy teenager who screams, "I hate you!" or "You ruined my life!" when you won't allow her to attend a party or wear that skirt that's twelve inches too short. A teenager who offers a snarky response for every question you ask.

This is the same person but with different perceptions of reality based on where this person is in life. One reality paints a picture of a loving infant. The other reality paints a picture of a mouthy teenager. But both portray the same individual, and as this person continues to grow and mature, the reality remains that this person is still, at the core of their being, the same and will continue to transform throughout the years.

A similar principle can be applied to our spouses. We begin with one perception—a googly-eyed, blissful love. This is removed within a two-year time frame, and our spouse may become more of a mouthy teenager, exerting his or her needs. As time progresses, so do you and your spouse. You grow, you learn, you understand one another on a deeper level, and just like it is with our children, the end result is hopefully two healthy, kind adults who appreciate the individuality that each brings to the relationship, with respect outweighing any annoying traits that may emerge. And maybe, just maybe, we can occasionally revisit utopia.

Happy Birthday! Celebrating Life

Our family has simple birthday celebrations. With eight children, we cannot afford (nor do we have the energy for) a big party for each individual. Instead, the birthday girl or guy gets a special day that includes a meal of their choice and Dad doing their chores. Whatever they request, I will make—within reason, of course. One child thought she'd try her luck and requested filet mignon. Not going to happen, sister. Some dinner go-to's have included lasagna, fettuccine alfredo, and biscuits and gravy, and homemade ice cream sandwiches usually top the choice for favorite dessert. And it's not only the kids who get excited about their special day; I'm usually bursting with anticipation as my birthday rolls around! I'm a sucker for presents, and Ryan often surprises me with the best gift I could ask for—a day off—but as my fortieth birthday inched closer and closer to becoming a reality, the typical excitement I usually had was lacking.

My maternal grandmother was in her forties when my mom gave birth to me. I had a two-year-old when I turned forty. It seemed like I was doing something backward. Some women love their forties, some not so much, and some merely tolerate these years. I fall in the group of toleration. We don't really have a choice, do we? We either age or we don't, but there was a significant shift in my body when I hit this magical number and the old adage "over the hill" really began to make sense. Sleep evaded my nights as hormones shifted. Wrinkles began to appear across my brow and around my eyes. My crooked mouth seemed even droopier, which, honestly, is my worst nightmare and may lead me to a plastic surgeon's office one of these days. Speaking of plastic surgery, maybe he or she could chop off the bulging pillow top around my waist that refuses to budge, no matter how many calories I restrict or sit-ups I crunch (which is zero if I'm being completely honest). My joints (even finger joints!) ache after a two-mile hike, and my rear end thickens with a pizza slice. However, for all the negatives, I am thankful. I am thankful for the blessing of another year. I am thankful for the moments I have to watch my children grow and mature and roll their eyes when I annoy them—which is more often than not lately. I am thankful for the wonderful relationships I have with my husband, friends, and family, and I am blessed to cultivate that which I love: working the soil with my hands, walking my achy body, writing words that will impact a weary world, and speaking words of encouragement for tired caregivers.

Life is a tremendous gift that I often take for granted. We all do! It's easy to become complacent and, sadly, that complacency is often jolted through pain and tragedy. I've been there. As Jason fought for his life, I vowed to never take the blessing of health for granted again, and I've tried to live this truth. However, it's a daily struggle to live in light of eternity and focus on what truly matters, letting go of insignificant concerns: money, belongings our money can buy, drama, Instagram land, keeping up with the Joneses and the Browns and the Walcotts. When we truly grasp that it's mostly a façade, the noise we tune into every day, we instead turn our attention to what really matters: moments with our loved ones; moments such as floating in the pool with family, maybe climbing on Ryan's shoulders and playing chicken with the teenagers and their friends and then paying for it dearly the next day with aches and pains; making homemade pizzas and topping the crust with sauce cultivated from vine-ripened tomatoes and deep-green peppers, both harvested from Dad's garden that morning; relaxing with Ryan on the patio after another solid day of accomplishments; tossing the chickens some corn with my little girl, my baby, who has most assuredly put every wrinkle on my face; the little moments that eventually make up a life well lived.

Each year I'm blessed with, there's a choice to be made. I can choose to dwell in the muck, the pain, the blended drama, the grief, Lucas's limitations, and the unfairness that Jason isn't here to raise his four children, or I can choose thankfulness. Notice the word *dwell*. There is a time of acknowledgment and diving into the pain; a time to really wrestle with the Almighty for a spell; the hardship, grief, custody battles, and cancer diagnosis. But then there's a choice. Will I choose to set up camp here—in the unfairness of the hand I was dealt, wallowing in grief—or will I choose to move into a place of growth that is obtained through a concerted effort to focus on gratefulness?

It's always a perception. I can focus on the past: how much better or worse it was, the loss incurred with death or divorce, the mangled and tangled and twisted emotions. Or I can focus on what I've gained: a new life, a spouse, lessons learned, and adopted children. It's that simple.

TAKEAWAYS

- One trick to disengaging from potential drama is to allow whatever the thought may be (*Susie's marriage seems so perfect!* or *Betty's always posting pictures of her well-behaved children on Instagram.*) to enter my mind only once; then, just as purposefully, I release those thoughts into God's hands; and then (one more step!) I tangibly move toward a life-giving activity such as walking, yoga, swimming, or cooking.

- I find it's helpful in my quest toward thankfulness to make a list, which I create on my birthday, when I have the day off. My list looks something like this: I'm thankful I have someone to share my life with. I'm thankful that God entrusted these dear children to my care. I'm thankful that my story has been redeemed and he has been faithful to see me through. I'm thankful for our health. I'm thankful for the beauty from the ashes—even if that beauty is layered with wrinkles.

Healthy-ish Carrot Cake

Ryan always makes my favorite dessert on my birthday—carrot cake! Here's a healthier take on this classic recipe that I could devour in a day if I truly decided to live life to the fullest (and then maybe I'd have no more life to live!). I swap out the oil for applesauce and the sugar for maple syrup. This cake is moist, full of flavor, bursting with carrots and pecans, and it is truly divine. I don't mess with the frosting—that would take the health agenda a bit too far.

- 1 cup maple syrup
- ¾ cup coconut oil, warmed and cooled
- ½ cup applesauce
- 4 eggs
- 3 cups shredded carrots
- 2½ cups flour

- 2 tsp cinnamon
- 2½ tsp baking soda
- 1 cup chopped pecans

Mix the first three ingredients together. Add the eggs. Mix well. Add the carrots and mix. Combine the flour, cinnamon, and baking soda, and slowly add to the liquids. Mix well. Stir in the pecans. Grease 3 cake pans, and bake at 350 degrees for about 20 minutes. Let the cake cool before frosting (see below).

Cream Cheese Frosting

- 1 stick of butter
- 1 package cream cheese
- 1 tsp vanilla extract
- 24 ounces powdered sugar
- 1 cup chopped pecans

Mix the first two ingredients well. Add vanilla. Mix. Add sugar slowly. Mix well and then add the pecans.

Mother's Day Anguish: Making Memories That Work for the New Family

Mother's Day arrives every year without fail, and this memorable day is laced with loads of emotion for many. Some grieve the loss of a mother, whether literally or figuratively; others rejoice in the wonderful relationship they have with their mother or a mother-like figure; and still others, like myself, agonize over the numerous complexities this day presents.

Ryan will inquire, every year, "How do you want your day to look?"

I usually reply, "My deepest desire is to enjoy a bubble bath without one single person asking or telling me anything through the door—a good thirty minutes is all I ask." (But then that would make me *not* a mother, right?)

Usually, this day is okay—peaceful, solid, void of any huge amounts of drama, as everyone is a bit on edge trying to make me feel special or scrambling to create a unique gift so that it doesn't look like they completely forgot. But this day is also a constant reminder of a gigantic ache for three of my children, and that makes it difficult and bittersweet. We try not to dwell on the agony of our past tragedies. We share memories with our children about Mom and Dad in heaven, we recognize their grief, and we respect their conflicted feelings on this day. Ryan and I do our best to model joy and not use the past as a crutch. Horrific events did occur, but we move forward in praise for what we have been given. We recognize that this life is fleeting and acknowledge God's faithfulness.

When my biological children were younger, they would embrace Mother's Day with joy and giddiness, and shower me with 500 billion homemade cards and pictures. As they've aged, this has changed, and now Mother's Day involves last-minute runs to Dollar General to purchase a card and Milk Duds—Caleb's go-to gift for me. Yes, I love Milk Duds. Generally, my adopted children are also excited about what the day represents and fully participate; however, I know that the day is also a painful reminder of what they've lost. One Mother's Day, this loss was extremely evident in the behavior of one of my children, who was not at all excited to celebrate the holiday.

This child was angry and had been for a week, and I noticed the angst every time a commercial aired about the upcoming day. The other kids would run to make me some thrown-together picture declaring their love, or they would hurry outside to pick another beautiful bunch of weeds, but this child would sit quietly, not meeting my eyes, not saying a word, just silently aching because of the loss. And I didn't know how to make it better.

I couldn't make it better, and that is incredibly difficult as a mother. My momma heart wanted to fix the hurt somehow, to be enough—so much so that the loss wouldn't sting, and in numerous ways, I knew I was a good mom, but it didn't erase the ache and how this day was a blatant reminder of that pain. As a mom, I wanted to take away the agony, take away the void, maybe even erase the memories because then it wouldn't be so painful, but I couldn't. I couldn't because at times I questioned God's decision in the matter. As a biological mother, I have a difficult time understanding why he would choose another woman over the mother who gave birth to Tate, Mya, and Jada and loved them. Who wanted them. It doesn't seem like the best decision, but then God's ways are not my ways, and he doesn't owe me an explanation. It only makes sense that his ways are higher than I can comprehend, and I don't believe that our comfort is always a top priority here on earth. No, I believe that our comfort often takes a back seat to his ultimate plan or purpose. And I believe that his plan probably resembles an adoption proceeding more than a biological conception—a choice to love others as ourselves rather than an instinctual connection, a choice to love God and choose his ways over our sinful nature that yearns to have everything our own way, a choice to lay down our lives and become more Christlike to those we live with.

This child and I got into a spat the night before Mother's Day, as we do occasionally, since we both view the world in a similar way, with a black-and-white tendency that needs to be right and each of us storing up arguments to match that desire. There was outright disobedience—something that had never occurred before. We aired our frustrations and mourned our losses and reaffirmed our love for one another, and I held my child and offered reassurance of my love, saying that I would continue to strive to be the best mom I could possibly be.

And isn't that all we can do for our children—those of our wombs and those of our hearts? Simply be the best we can be for each individually and collectively, relying on God's grace and mercy as we stumble and then pick ourselves back up. We pray that somehow the pain and loss and ache will be gone one day, and it will make perfect sense when we end our race here on earth and come face-to-face with the One who orchestrated it all, our Abba Father who has graciously adopted each of us into his eternal family.

TAKEAWAYS

- It is what it is. Whether it's Mother's Day or some other holiday that doesn't feel the same anymore, mourn the change, grieve the loss, and then embrace it for what it is.
- Simplify. I'm done with expectations I place on myself and others on Mother's Day. I'm totally over it because I always feel disappointed. My favorite Mother's Day memory is when I woke up one Sunday morning—the Mother's Day after I miscarried—and declared that I wasn't in the mood for church and, instead, we were going roller-skating. Yep, all nine of us went, even Lucas who was much younger then, and it was a total blast. We had no expectations, outside of having fun. Allow yourself permission to define what works for your new family as you move forward, and remember, there is no rule book.
- Get over the expectations of others. Following up on the second point: You do you and your family. Don't worry about what others think.

- Shower yourself with grace. There may be heaviness for a while as you acclimate to the new normal, but this is okay. Time really does heal many wounds, and it will get easier.

Mya will often make these super simple cinnamon rolls on Mother's Day, and I will wake up in the morning to the glorious cinnamon scent wafting through the house. Add a few pieces of bacon, and I'm in heaven.

- ½ cup honey
- 2 cups lukewarm water
- 1½ tbsp active dry yeast
- 1½ tsp salt
- ¼ cup olive oil
- 5 cups bread flour
- ½–1 cup flaxseeds, wheat germ, or chia seeds
- 1 stick of butter, melted
- Cinnamon and sugar, to taste

Add honey to the water. Stir with a fork. Add the yeast. Stir. Let proof for ten minutes. Add the salt and oil. Mix. Slowly add the bread flour and flaxseeds, wheat germ, or chia seeds. Mix well. Knead for 5–8 minutes. Let rest in a well-oiled bowl for about an hour.

Roll out into a rectangle on a floured surface. Spread melted butter over the surface. Sprinkle cinnamon and sugar on top of the butter. Roll up the dough and cut it into 1–2-inch pieces (depending on how big you like your rolls). Place in buttered 9×13 pans and cover with towels. Let rise until doubled in size. Cook at 350 degrees for about 15–20 minutes until lightly browned. Cool and then ice.

Icing

- 1-2 tbsp melted butter
- 4-5 cups powdered sugar
- 1 tsp maple flavoring
- 1-2 tsp coffee
- A few tbsp almond milk

Whisk all ingredients to a pourable consistency and drizzle all over the rolls.

Two Christmas Trees: Combining Traditions to Secure Connections

I love Christmas. The warmth of the crackling fire on Christmas Eve as we open gifts, Lucas deeply entrenched in satisfaction as he sways his head to the pounding rhythm of the Trans-Siberian Orchestra belting out favorites on our overhead speakers, inhaling the scent of fresh cinnamon rolls and bacon on Christmas morning, and the soft white snow slowly falling outside—although I haven't enjoyed much snow since I left Michigan!

I love the traditions that the holiday ushers in and gathering with friends and family who we don't see often. I also love how Christmas signals the birth of new beginnings and how hope becomes personified through the arrival of the Christ child—hope found in a manger in Bethlehem, hope that situations will improve, hope that we can lose that extra ten pounds when the calendar flips over to the new year, hope that life might possibly change.

Ryan and I were in full anticipation mode about our hope-filled future in 2011—the year we were married, as the prior two years had been drenched in painful memories. Jason had not felt well in 2009 as chemotherapy and radiation pounded away at his body, and although he was determined to work, anything that required physical strength was becoming increasingly more difficult as time marched on. His job opportunities were scarce, and we struggled to stay afloat financially in the middle of a mild economic fallout. We were a family of six, and he stubbornly remained proactive, taking any jobs that were available, including a part-time position at a local holistic center and subbing at the public school when jobs became available.

On December 24, 2009, Jason received an unexpected email stating that his position was terminated at the holistic doctor's office. We were already struggling to make ends meet, and I had no idea how we were going to pay our bills with this blow to our budget. I was even more concerned about how we would provide any Christmas gifts for our four children. Thankfully, they were young, and as they opened their used gifts that I had been able to find at a local second-hand store, they squealed in delight—although Caleb has since informed me that he knew the gifts were used but didn't care because Dad had cancer. Cue the tears . . .

As I opened my gifts, I remember calculating how much income a return would provide. Most of my gifts did find their way to the return counter that year and were exchanged for either gift cards that could be used for necessities or cash that would be used to pay our bills. December 2010 was also difficult. Jason had passed away that August, and I met Ryan for the first time two weeks before Christmas day. I wrestled with feelings of guilt, anger, sadness, joy, elation, and euphoria as I dealt with the conflicting emotions of falling in love with one man and mourning the death of the man I had been in love with for ten years. That year also became a beautiful reflection of hope as a local church surprised us with a truck full of gifts on Christmas Eve for my fatherless children, and this act of selfless love provided them with one of the best Christmas experiences they had seen in years.

Now, here we were, newly married in 2011, a year brimming with hope, possibilities, and beginnings: decorations and cookie decorating and gifts galore and . . . conflicting traditions. I hadn't seen that issue coming. I assumed as mom and wife that I would orchestrate Christmas as I had always done, but when Ryan pulled out his Christmas bins from his previous life, and I pulled out my Christmas bin, it was obvious that our cultures and traditions would also need some time to blend.

My bin was filled to the brim with beautiful gold and dusty rose ornaments—decor for the Victorian era. His bins looked like fruit loops and an array of rainbow colors, red, orange, yellow, green, blue, and purple, greeted me as I lifted the lids open—not my style.

I stared at the contents—a little bit concerned about being respectful but not sure how I was going to say, "I don't really like these ornaments."

A discussion ensued, and we arrived at a compromise that we both felt comfortable with that first Christmas.

We set up two Christmas trees—one representing his past life and one representing mine. One overflowing with bright and colorful decorations; the other with peaceful Victorian décor. Both represented our family.

This new tradition didn't last long (only a year, in fact), as we discovered that two trees required a lot of work—more work than we wanted to undertake during the holidays—and two trees also wasn't the most economical decision for a family of nine. As time went on and we settled into our roles, I did become the orchestrator of the holidays as our reality became less about two separate families and more about our new big family.

One of our traditions has always been unwrapping gifts on Christmas Eve. There's something soothing about the dark night sky littered with stars (and possibly a few snowflakes), and this tradition has included one of our favorite meals, English Muffin buns, a meal I grew up with, and an easy option to throw together after the gifts have been unwrapped and everyone has settled into exploring their new toys. I honestly don't know if my mom formulated the recipe or if she found it somewhere, but these are addictive little morsels. They may seem strange (believe me, every new in-law initially recoils in disgust), but they are soon requesting them just like the rest of us! These can be made a day or two ahead, which also makes them convenient for the holidays, and the leftovers (if there are any!) reheat beautifully.

- Package of English muffins
- Butter
- Cream cheese with chives
- Provolone cheese
- Deli ham

Heat the oven to 350 degrees. Split open each English muffin and spread a thin layer of butter on top. Add another thin layer of cream cheese, then a piece of ham, and finish with a slice of cheese. Bake until lightly browned and the cheese is bubbling—about 15 minutes.

12

JUST KEEP LIVIN'

Choosing *Joy* in Your *New Life*

When I met Ryan for the first time, I was 5'9" and 125 pounds, dripping wet. The years of stress had taken a toll as I cared for Jason and our young children—a toll on my mental and emotional well-being for sure, but dang my body was looking pretty good (my idea of "good" being extremely thin). During the months leading up to Jason's death, I rarely ate as I was constantly on the go, nursing an infant, throwing a load of laundry into the washing machine, administering medications, and then stopping back in the laundry room to dry, fold, and put away clothes. I might grab a handful of potato chips in between the never-ending to-do list, maybe a small salad, or dip a cracker in hummus on my way to changing another diaper. Not highly nutritious but apparently a pretty effective way to lose weight.

Fast-forward a few years, a few years since that initial meeting in Savannah, and I do not look the same. I have gained a bit of poundage. Happiness, the absence of hospice, age, hormones, and the baby I had at thirty-eight years old have all contributed to this weight gain, and speaking of that baby (bless her heart), that experience changed my body more than all the other pregnancies combined! I now have an excessive amount of scar tissue jiggling around my waist, which led to an entire wardrobe change after her birth. Form-fitting clothes have been replaced with draping shawls. Skinny jeans with sweat pants. I wish I could say that I always have peace about my body, but I haven't made it there yet. Just when I think I may finally be to the point of acceptance, I'll change my clothes in front of Ryan on the wrong day of the month, and I imagine that the sight of my jiggly middle laced with scar tissue makes him want to dry heave. He tells me I have a very active imagination and that this scenario has never crossed his mind.

I've always had a love/hate relationship with my body, but my second marriage triggered a comparison critic that I've worked hard to overcome. Ryan and I both married young the first time around. Let me preface the next thing I say with this truth—growing old is a gift. I believe this in the depth of my soul, but while Jason and Kaci remain forever young and beautiful in the hearts and minds of everyone, Ryan and I continue to age. I continue to age! He doesn't care. I have a difficult time not caring as I become saggier and more wrinkly and grayer with each passing year.

I've been able to combat some of these negative thoughts by focusing on the amazing accomplishments my body has completed through the years. This is a body that never let go of Lucas—even when the specialists said it was only a matter of time. My body hung on to that precious boy's life with every ounce of strength it had. My body made enough milk to exclusively breastfeed him for the first six months of his life. My body nursed four other babies for at least a year and the last one—well, for quite some time (three years to be exact). My body never gave up when it required an immediate blood transfusion after the birth of Annabelle. It nurtured and protected five babies in the womb and continues to nurture and protect eight children outside of the womb. My body laid beside a man for days and provided comfort and strength as he passed from one world to the next. My body stood beside another man and his three motherless children and vowed to love, honor, and cherish them. My body is strong. It is able to bathe a sixteen-year-old teenage boy, lift him in and out of the van when he's being stubborn, and carry him off the bus at the end of a school day. My body is wrinkled and squishier than it used to be, but my oh my, the stories these cells could tell.

Today, at forty-three years old, I eat healthy, walk, and practice yoga, but the weight still refuses to budge. It makes no sense. I have to choose to focus on how I feel and how my clothes fit, rather than obsessing about a number. Here are a couple of tried-and-true methods that I've found to be effective in my journey toward body acceptance.

- If I wouldn't say it about someone else, why do I say it about myself? Isn't that the truth? We say horrible things to ourselves that would never ever cross our lips about someone else—well, maybe a few people, since we're only human—but really, self-love starts with ourselves.
- Accept a compliment. It drives Ryan bonkers when he tells me I look nice, and I immediately reply, "Oh gosh, I look fat." He became downright angry once when he offered a compliment and was immediately snuffed with my rebuke. He then informed me that either I was going to learn to accept his compliments or he was going to stop giving them.

- Our daughters are watching us. I have four precious girls, and two have entered their teenage years. I sometimes gasp in horror as I hear them talk about their bodies. I shamefully admit, *I did that*. Not entirely, but I had a hand in how they see themselves.
- Consistency is key. I strive to eat clean 80 percent of the time. I try not to gorge on Milk Duds and Cheetos on a consistent basis. I do allow myself occasional treats—a glass of wine, a wedge of cheese, or some prosciutto on real, gluttonous bread. It works best for me to not eat until about 11:00 a.m. My first meal is usually a green smoothie, which I've perfected, and then I'll eat clean and light until six o'clock and allow myself whatever we're having for dinner. Because I don't indulge heavily throughout the day, my capacity to eat a lot at six o'clock is diminished, but by allowing myself to eat whatever I want, I feel like I'm not being deprived. We need to trick ourselves sometimes.
- Movement. I walk two miles every morning. Again, consistency is key. Make whatever movement you enjoy a part of your life. I also incorporate about twenty minutes of yoga every night. I found that I wouldn't commit to yoga if I didn't have an hour, and then I would go weeks without doing it at all. The remedy was to do what I could. Twenty minutes is very attainable after dinner, and it is a relaxing way to usher in bedtime.

Green Smoothie

I love sipping on this smoothie as the first meal of my day. It's light, full of nutrition, and provides a burst of energy mid-morning.

- A handful of spinach
- 1 cup pineapple

- ½ cup coconut water
- 1 cup almond milk
- ½ cup yogurt
- ½ cup blueberries
- Whatever else you want to add

Blend everything until smooth. Enjoy!

(Don't forget, if you're enjoying these recipes, you can find them all available for print on my website: www.jessplusthemess.com /blendedrecipes.)

Cleo: Persevering in Life

Cleo has been beside me through everything during the past twenty years. Cleo is my cat—my very old lady cat as we speak. Jason and I adopted her after she was weaned from her momma in 2000, after we said *I do*. A pet seems to be the natural progression for couples—perhaps like giving the idea of children a test run before committing to a real live human being.

Cleo rode along happily in our car when Jason and I moved to Detroit, and then moved back out of the city after we changed our minds six months later. She was there when we temporarily lived with my parents, and still there when we moved into our first home—a modular trailer down the road from my folks. She remained steady with the move to an apartment during an interim period as we built our dream house and stayed beside me as I desperately prayed for my unborn baby to live. She was there when we brought Lucas home for the first time, and remained steadfast with the move into our new house—even after the birth of Mabel, when she became more of an outdoor cat and slept in the garage at night. She laid beside Jason during his final days, purring him to sleep and comforting me as I mourned. She embraced baby Joshua and soon three more siblings who would carry her upside down, pull her tail, dress her up in baby-doll clothes, and push her in a baby stroller. She was tolerant of it all. She continued her excursions through life with another move in Michigan, a move to rural Tennessee, and most recently a move to the city, which has to feel a bit like a retirement paradise after her rural encounters.

I am not an animal person, and I don't typically become attached to pets. When I visit extended family and their dog or cat begins to make its way toward my lap, the owners have been known to say, "Get down! Jess won't like that," which is typically true. I don't want a dog or a cat sitting on me or nuzzling me or licking me. And I don't really want to take care of one more breathing entity. Maybe it's because I live with an overabundance of human beings and private space is a hot commodity that's difficult to come by? Maybe it's due to my time being stretched so thin that I don't want one more thing on my to-do list? Maybe.

But with Cleo it's different.

When we first moved to Tennessee, she was still active and brought us special treats and laid them at the foot of our front door: birds, lizards, and mice. She even tolerated the addition of five more cats, two by choice and three through an unexpected pregnancy of a sister cat.

One early morning, she emerged from the woods limping and mangled, attacked by a wild animal, fur torn out in patches, skinny, frail, and obviously shaken up. We brought her in and set up a space in the garage where she could recuperate. Our boys snuck her into their beds at night, which we allowed because we felt sorry for her. We were sure this was her end, but it wasn't. She completely healed within a few weeks but was never quite the same. After her last encounter with a wild beast, she learned her lesson and never ventured far from the safety of our house again. She knew that if she did, she might not return.

She's tired, but she's full of grit, and you can still see the fight in her dim, glassy eyes. She no longer brings us special treats or waits for our approval before eating them. She doesn't eat much of anything anymore and never leaves the comfort of our covered patio. Ryan even has a soft spot for her and showed up with a heated cat home last winter from Tractor Supply. She can be found in it most days, purring away in contented bliss. She is aware of her diminished capacity, and she honors that awareness. We are also aware that our days with her are numbered, and we cater to her whims. I sneak her salmon and tuna, and I take time to pet her old bones. She purrs deeply and closes her eyes—knowing that I will be there until she decides she's had enough. I do believe it will be a decision, and I will deeply mourn her when she breathes her last. Part of me mourns already because I believe her pride might not even allow us to be a part of it. I fear she'll leave and die in dignity, sparing us the pain of having to watch her suffer.

What a life she's led. The tenacity. The fight. The experiences. The moves, the deaths, the children, the struggles. Talk about a "just keep livin'" cat.

I want to be a Cleo—fighting when I need to, adapting when the situation requires it, never giving up or giving in, persevering through difficult times but owning an awareness of my need for rest, for peace, and for God's hand to loving stroke my head as I do hers.

The Elephant: Learning to Trust God's Plan

A few years ago, we traded in our minivan with numerous bells and whistles—television, remote-controlled seats, and DVD players—for a van that was completely new to us. A former church van found on Craigslist—found after scouring the ads for months. A long, gray, extended, fantastic deal of a van. A vehicle we didn't currently need but were believing we would soon require with the arrival of a new baby. A baby who had yet to be conceived. A van that reminded me of the embarrassment I suffered as a child while riding in something similar with my seven siblings—something almost exactly like our new purchase. I vividly recall the embarrassment I felt as a teenager watching my three younger brothers plaster their faces against the long, bus-like windows, pretending we were on an outing from the nearby insane asylum. And now, here I was, a mother of seven children, choosing a vehicle exactly like the one I despised in my childhood. What was I doing to my poor children?

We purchased the van, despite my trepidation over what it would do to my offspring's mental and emotional well-being, and affectionately named it *The Elephant*, in its big, gray, no-nonsense glory.

It's funny how God works.

I always dreamt of four kids, which is exactly what I got until God's plan unraveled and my responsibilities practically doubled overnight. The addition of three more mouths to feed would have sent many women into a complete panic, and believe me, I don't always handle the situation gracefully, but raising a bushel of children does, in a strange way, feel like a natural extension of who I am, and I suppose it is in the grand scheme of life.

I was born to my parents, Jim and Tammy, in 1977, the first child of what would become a large family of fourteen. I was raised with tons of structure and discipline, and in an environment where I was able to glean invaluable skills that serve me well as a mom of eight. Skills such as gardening, baking, food preservation, and chore-chart management. And now, here I am, cruising along in our big ole elephant of a van with eight kids, thankful God ordained it from the beginning of time.

Ryan's Take

Jess and I were raised in different environments with different expectations, but God was also preparing me for a future with her and our eight children. When I was around five years old, a new family moved in next door, a family of six with a mom and dad and four kids. I was curious when I learned that two of the children had severe special needs, a boy and a girl—older than me and somewhat scary because of the unknown. The oldest boy was twice my size, and he would wobble around, unsteady on his feet. When he became agitated, he would bang his head against anything that was nearby. They were my neighbors for about twelve years, and during that time, I grew accustomed to my special-needs friend's unusual behaviors and learned to help calm him down. I would also attempt to get them both involved in our neighborhood play and try to get the other kids to welcome them.

When I met Lucas, he didn't scare me because of my past experiences, and I felt comfortable being with him. As he grasped at my hands and tried licking me and figuring out who I was in his unique ways, I'm sure Jess was about to crawl out of her skin, but God prepared me many years earlier, so that Lucas wasn't a deal breaker. Not even close. In fact, I saw it as a sign that I was supposed to be his new dad, as he needed someone like me to be there for him. I love Lucas like he is my own flesh and blood, and he loves me in his own way.

In my first marriage, Kaci began to feel like we needed to adopt a family in need. Yes, a family—not a child or two, but a whole litter of kids. I was not on board but agreed, hoping my heart would change. We had just spent the last twenty months as volunteer missionaries in Albania and were feeling confused about what to do next. We considered becoming a live-in foster family in a community, which meant our family of five would live in a house with up to eight foster children. This idea terrified me, but I wasn't very adept at communicating. We explored this option for months but discovered that most foster communities only allowed two biological children, and we had three. With that door closed, we returned to considering adoption and began classes. I was not excited but agreed nonetheless. With the classes completed, we had to make difficult decisions about what kind of children we were willing to share our lives with. I was now officially on board after witnessing the abuse many of these kids had suffered and felt God leading us down this path. After entering our criteria, we received a list of potential candidates each month. I was shocked to see that there were entire families of children in desperate need of a home—families as large as eight children whose parents were no longer in the picture—and no one was willing to adopt them. My family was about to double or even triple in size, and I was scared to death.

Three months passed, and each time we would choose a family to move forward with, something went wrong. During those three months, Kaci's headaches intensified, and she began questioning why God would put this on her heart and then repeatedly take it away. In March 2010, Kaci's headaches led to a diagnosis of a brain tumor, and our plans to adopt were set aside as we focused on her healing. I remember looking back on those days and thinking, *Why? Why would we feel led to adopt when God already knew our outcome?* Now I understand. I finalized the adoption of Jess's four children in 2013.

When people say God works in mysterious ways, it makes me smile. I'm amazed to realize how many events occurred in my life to prepare me for my current reality. God knew Lucas was destined to be my son, and he prepared me to have a big family. I choose to believe they weren't coincidences, and I know I am fulfilling God's call on my life.

As we walk through confusing times, we must remember that we don't always get to see the end result; however, it is our job to walk in obedience—step by step—and trust that God's hand will guide us to the end. He is faithful to use all things for good for those who believe. This doesn't mean it will all be used for good according to what our definition of good looks like—nope, sorry. My definition of good did not involve a son with profound special needs, but I see today that it is God's perfect definition of goodness, and Lucas is completely healed and whole in the way that God created him to be. Neither Ryan nor I saw our definition of good as losing our spouses, but God's ways were higher than ours and everything in creation is called to bring glory to his name—including our lives. Joy derives from faithful obedience. When we are faithful, he will work all things according to his perfect plan—not ours. Take heart in that promise if you are walking through confusing or tumultuous terrains. Continue moving forward. Step by step and moment by moment, he will direct your path.

The Cloud Is Moving: Recognizing the Need for Change

It takes courage to say that a certain way of operating isn't working anymore, and truthfully, our rural life in Tennessee hadn't been working for a while by the time we were brave enough to step away.

In 2013, we left Michigan for a dream that included a simple life in rural Tennessee. This is how Ryan and I operate—we hear

Go! and we go. We married quickly, Ryan moved to Michigan within months of proposing, and we moved to Tennessee after seeing our future homestead once. We found childcare and drove ten hours to our recently purchased dilapidated house, with our travel trailer firmly hooked to the back of our vehicle. Our two-week goal was to make our new digs livable—which it was not by a long shot! We painted and laid carpet and fixed pipes and killed oodles of bugs and registered kids for school and then wiped our brows and returned home, only to reload a few days later and head south for good. We never looked back. We are decisive, informed, and not prone to obsessing about how our decisions would be perceived by others. To reference a biblical metaphor, we move with the cloud: "If the cloud did not lift, they did not set out—until the day it lifted" (Exod. 40:37).

Our new, large, potentially beautiful house overlooked the Tennessee River with the most breathtaking thirty acres of land but required a complete renovation. We immediately got to work and began building a simple life with our family. We worked hard. Really hard. Ryan renovated more than 5,000 square feet of house with pure grit and his own two hands. He added bedrooms and bathrooms and worked magic with the red clay dirt. We learned how to garden and raise chickens and brew kombucha and feed sourdough starters and bake the perfect brick-oven pizza. YouTube was our faithful teacher, and we devoured the knowledge she offered.

We joyfully added our last child, Annabelle, in 2015—a dream come true as Ryan and I prayed about having a child together. I wrote a book, finished a master's degree, and obtained a teaching job at a local college. When we desperately needed resources for Lucas, as a true firstborn Enneagram 1 Reformer, I started The Lucas Project—a nonprofit organization that provides recognition, resources, and respite for special-needs families.

We've sung and celebrated and mourned and fought and screamed and loved and lived and danced in the rain with bubbles trickling down our bellies when the old copper pipes burst. Our life was joy filled. Our life was hard. It was soul changing, and it served a purpose by solidifying us as a family. And then, one day, the grace was gone, and it was time to say goodbye to our rural life. *A reason for a season*, as my wise former pastor would say.

The transition had been simmering for about two years and intensified to the point of tangibly taking steps to look at properties after Ryan's numerous health scares during the summer of 2017. We realized we could no longer continue running on a hamster wheel of isolation with eight children. Every doctor's appointment, grocery run, eye doctor, dentist, restaurant, church, school activity, yoga, gym, sick kid at school, Wednesday-night church, hardware store, school drop-off, respite days, library—they were all thirty minutes away, minimum. And then thirty minutes back. Times ten people. Times two towns. Times a Lucas, who doesn't like new experiences or long car rides. Times—it was too much. Our reality caused us to become angry and isolated and panicky and clinging to each other for dear life, rather than relying on other people for help.

We became desperate for community, like a fish desperate for water, but it couldn't happen where we were. We were too far away, with too many hurdles to make it a reality.

We searched for help. Childcare, house cleaning, plumbing, maintenance, carpet laying, everything and anything, but it wasn't readily available, and our house was not easily accessible, and so we gritted our teeth and bore the heavy burden. We took care of business like grown-ups do, and then we looked at each other one day and barely whispered what we had been thinking for some time: "We don't have to stay here." We spoke the truth that had been residing in our hearts, which became the first step toward change.

We did believe that rural Tennessee was our forever home, and we poured our souls into it like it was. We believed in our simple life with every cell in our weary bodies, and we still do in many ways, but not in rural America. Not in isolation. Not with eight children and special needs and severe autism. Not with teenagers who need social lives and activities. We need them to have activities so we don't have to bear all the eye rolls alone. Seriously. There can absolutely be too much togetherness—especially within the age group from around twelve to eighteen.

We knew the time had come to trade the physical beauty of our environment for messy, joy-filled community somewhere else. And as the whispers became loud vocalizations, we began the process of finding a community and a house, and we weren't exactly sure where this process would lead.

The criteria were strict. We wanted to downsize from our large home to something more manageable. We needed at least five bedrooms. We desired acreage in a neighborhood because we do still believe in a sustainable lifestyle. We wanted a mother-in-law suite for Lucas and his future aide (God willing). We wanted to be close to schools, a church with a special-needs ministry, and a gym. We wanted to be near a hospital just in case. We needed pizza delivery. We looked and looked, in town after town, and we were disappointed time and time again and then—I looked online one last time while I was in Michigan for a conference. I found what seemed to be the perfect home near Nashville and met our Realtor there on my return home. It was nearly perfect and reminded us of our current home. It had almost everything on our list of criteria. There was also a church a mile away with a special-needs ministry, a mother-in-law suite, and every pizza delivery option imaginable.

We purchased this house and moved in two months later—the day after Christmas in 2018. We are finally beginning to exhale, as our burdens have lifted slightly. Our family had been simmering away on the back of the stove, melding into this blended family without many distractions, and now it was time to join the feast of community. Rural life offers beauty in many ways, but the beauty had begun to suffocate as our needs shoved us further and further into isolation and rural America began to close in like a tomb.

In a way, it felt like failure to walk away from what we thought was our dream home. I'm the "just keep livin'" girl. I'm not a quitter, right? Wrong. I've been broken repeatedly in this life. Broken in good ways as I shed what no longer works or maybe never did. Rural life stripped me down to the shell of my being, and now I'm rebuilding that skeleton with new flesh—flesh that is ready to join others in community. Of course, there were sad goodbyes as we moved forward—goodbyes to people, experiences, and a house that was my home. I'll no longer be able to drink in the natural beauty as the early morning sun peeks through the clouds while I sip coffee on the porch. I'll no longer hear the coyotes howl throughout the night. I'll no longer be able to dance down my deserted dirt road, shaking my fist at the sky while singing at the top of my lungs, or fall to my knees during times of quiet desperation, lifting my face to the heavens, hidden among the trees. Sad goodbyes are a part of growth as they are a part of life. But the cloud moved and we, as we always do, will continue to move forward, step by step, into where he calls us. The next right decision.

Just Keep Livin': How Thankfulness Shifts Our Perspective

> *"The measure of obstacles we overcome is often a sign of the greatness waiting for us on the other side. When I reach my breaking point, I think of you and the obstacles you have overcome in your life, and it gives me strength."*
>
> —Ryan, 2012

When Ryan and I met in 2010, we were in a season of death, with the passing of our spouses Jason and Kaci, and this loss included a burial of lifelong dreams. Dreams of a nuclear, intact family. Expectations that we would grow old with our spouses. A dream of biological parents raising the children they chose to bring into this world, and the assumption that the biological father would walk his daughter down the aisle one day. Buckets of grief and despair and unmet opportunities filled our hearts.

During the next few years, we enjoyed a resurrection as our lives merged and birthed new realities: our marriage and blended family; a simple life in rural Tennessee, where we learned to work the hard clay earth with our bare hands, where the sun wrinkled our brows, and we slept deeply at night after a day's labor tending to children, chickens, housework, and gardens. A good life. A difficult life. A life where every moment was a teacher in some capacity. A life where I birthed a book, a teaching career, a nonprofit dream, and another child. Buckets of hope and growth and beauty.

As I grapple with these final words, I once again find myself in a season of decay and confusion, with our family enduring broken bodies over the past year: Ryan's shoulder surgery; my fractured foot, which continues to hinder my participation in favorite activities like walking, tennis, and yoga; and Lucas's brain surgeries, which resulted in his month-long admission on PICU in December 2019. As I write these words, my children have just reentered the craziest school year of their life after a five-month hiatus, where every part of me was broken as a pandemic swept across the world: my control, my plans, and my pride—nothing working out like I thought it would. And I still grapple with numerous unanswered questions and concerns about how the future is going to play out. *Will they stay in school? Is school good for them? Will they get sick?* Broken ideals and realities surround our family as we restructure and determine how we'll proceed from here. And through these trials, we've buried systems that used to work when the world was one way, and now they no longer serve us emotionally or spiritually, and we wait because we *know*.

I know because I've been here before. I remember August 2010, the most difficult month of my life, as a tumultuous month full of overwhelming obligations and demands—work, Lucas's birthday, family pictures, doctor's appointments, four children farmed out on a daily basis to anyone and everyone, the arrival of hospice equipment, nursing staff in and out, important phone calls requiring life-or-death decisions, and ultimately good-byes whispered and a funeral prepared for a young husband and father. I wait and I remember. I recall that this is familiar soil, deep and dark and rich soil where perhaps I've not been buried but have instead been planted, and now I await my reemergence into the light.

I wait for a resurrection.

And I am confident that growth will occur in due time because that's how the gig works. It's how our lives are rigged.

Everything remains in motion: a continuous movement of death and resurrection, waves upon waves washing away the brokenness and grief and moving what remains to the shore—natural disasters and despair and divorce and special needs and bereavement not excluded, an intricate blending of grit and grace. It's all involved, collectively and individually; ashes to beauty and back to ashes again; circular movements until the maestro sweeps his baton for the last time and bows his head in holy reverence; that moment when his beloved creation leans into the finality and releases a labored breath—bursting through the birth canal into an everlasting resurrection.

And until then?

We rise up out of the boat and walk toward the land; we walk toward the Rock of Ages where there is no shifting sand. We move toward a purpose higher than ourselves. We pursue life and do our darndest to live in the present and practice thankfulness. Loss has a way of bringing a newfound appreciation and respect for the present. There are lessons in despair that are incredibly painful, but these lessons are also remarkably life-giving as we navigate into a new reality where pain bequeaths joy.

Gratefulness has the ability to carry a family forward as they navigate the numerous roadblocks encountered to get to a healthy place of peace and fulfillment. I should preface—there's no set arrival date to this place of peace. The process will be ongoing until the day we die. Ryan would love it if I could just give him a future time when we will no longer struggle with anything and instead live in peace and harmony until the end of our days, but that's not how life works—not in a traditional family nor in a blended one. But we keep lifting ourselves up out of despair. Keep willing ourselves to rise out of the muck and put one foot in front of the other. We keep moving forward, one step at a time with determination, grit, and grace.

We just keep livin'.

ALL THE DELICIOUS, CROWD-PLEASING RECIPES FOUND IN

BLENDED WITH GRIT AND Grace

are available on beautiful recipe cards at
www.jessplusthemess.com/blendedrecipes.

CHICKEN CURRY

This dish is comfort food at its finest, especially during the cooler autumn and winter months, and it's full of healthy nutrients that will start your family off right during the cold and flu season. You'll feel like the parent of the year as you dole this out on your family's plates.

INGREDIENTS

1 large onion, diced
4–5 garlic cloves, diced
Olive oil
1–2 large jalapeños, diced (remove seeds for less spice)
2 28-ounce cans of chopped tomatoes
4–5 chicken thighs, cut into pieces
7–8 cups of chicken or bone broth
2 cans of chickpeas, drained and rinsed
1–2 tbsp curry powder
1 tbsp cumin
1 tsp chili powder
Salt and pepper to taste

METHOD

1. Sauté the onion and garlic with the olive oil on medium heat until translucent.
2. Add the jalapeños and cook for a minute—stirring constantly.
3. Add the tomatoes and broth. Stir.
4. Add the remaining ingredients.
5. Stir and simmer on low all day long, stirring occasionally.
6. Serve over rice or a baked potato.

You can print them for free and
add them to your family's favorite recipes.